Parable of a Broken Heart

A Guidebook for Surviving Separation and Divorce

Steph Leis

Centre Stage Publishing

ISBN: 978-0-9920942-1-8 (Paperback)

Privacy: For privacy reasons, some names, locations, and dates may have been changed.

Cover and Interior Design by STOKE Publishing

Illustrations by Steph Leis

Ordering Information: Special discounts are available on quantity purchases. For details on bulk purchases for your group, please contact the author via email at steph@stephleis.com.

ParableOfABrokenHeart.com

To all the women and men feeling so incredibly heartbroken, rejected, abandoned, and alone. To those suffering through a separation and divorce and have lost so much of your identity, family, friends, dreams, and hope. You are stronger than you know. This feeling will not last forever, you will be happy again.

I promise <3

God is within her, she will not fall.

Psalm 46:5

Contents

Introduction vii

1. The End 1
2. Alone 9
3. Time and Space to Heal 19
4. Quick Happiness Fixes 27
5. Simple Reminders 35
6. Hiring Your Besties 43
7. Who Am I? 49
8. Reality Pause 59
9. Create a Safe Space 71
10. What Else You Lose 79
11. Feeling Those Firsts 89
12. Forgiveness 97
13. Funeral for My Past 103
14. Mental Health is Not for the Weak 109
15. When You're Ready 115
16. Listen for the Lessons 123
17. Writing Your Next Chapter 127

Epilogue 131

Acknowledgments 133

Resources 135

About the Author 137

what if our *love stories* are not
about our lovers but are the
tales of how we found ourselves

l.e. bowman

Introduction

Mantra: *Just breathe.*

He left me, and he left me so incredibly broken.

Broken, shattered, and crushed.

I had disintegrated into dust. Floating around with no purpose, no reason, no motivation. Just merely existing, without a clue of how I could ever come back together again.

The one decision that was out of my control and I had lost it all. My husband, my lover, my best friend, my home, my hopes and dreams, my future, my family. Gone. And I was so completely lost and alone.

We didn't have the perfect marriage. We fought, we didn't communicate well, we made other things or people priorities over each other and life got tough. It took me a long time to share the blame with him, that him leaving me wasn't all my fault. It was decisions and choices over our six-year marriage on both of our ends that led our marriage to this. But I loved hard, and I loved that man more than I ever thought possible, and that is something I will never regret.

Being a good Christian girl, I didn't, and still don't, believe in divorce. At least not in a marriage where a little work, effort, and choosing each other could have helped us pull through. I thought we could get through anything. I was fully committed to the holy sacrament of the vows I took on our wedding day. Even after he said the words, "I want a separation," I continued to love hard, never giving up the tiniest bit of hope that he might change his mind and come home to us.

Growing up I was a hard-core romantic. I would cry listening to love songs like All My Life by K-Ci & JoJo, and was obsessed with the Twilight saga. I couldn't wait to find my Edward. It's all I wanted. To find and spend my life with the love of my life, have a family, and live happily ever after. Because it was that easy, right?

I felt so completely lucky and blessed to have found my person at such a young age and I couldn't wait to start forever with him. We started dating while I was on my summer break back home in small town Saskatchewan before going into my fourth and final year of my bachelor's degree. I was living on the other side of the country and we did our first eight months of our relationship long-distance. When I moved back home to be with him after graduation, we swore that our long-distance relationship gave us a strong foundation and we would never take each other for granted. We were engaged, and got married on our two year dating anniversary, shortly after I turned 23.

I was obsessed. He was like a drug to me, and I couldn't get enough of him. These days there's a name for that—co-dependence, but back then we were just young and so in love. And that flame of love burned strong and had a good, long run.

But being young and in love can also mean I didn't have the time to individually develop emotional intelligence, strong communication skills, or any relationship experience on how to deal with the hard stuff that life throws your way in order to properly support one another as a partner should.

Love is blind. So incredibly blind. Love shines over the darkness, masking issues and problems that in time turn into bigger challenges, eventually forming cracks between a couple. That is the story of my eight years with him. A combination of the brightest lights and the darkest shadows.

Which is why when he left me, I died inside. Because without him, I was nothing. And it took me a LONG ass time to find myself again.

Divorce is incredibly common in our modern world. I am in complete awe just imagining how many people have gone through the same kind of heartbreak as I have. Every marriage and every divorce is different, but I've found that because it is so common, in North America particularly, it is widely undermined how painful the transition is from *we* to *me* and is often not given the proper grace and time needed to heal.

Divorce Is A Grieving Process.

It's death to life as you know it. The plans, the dreams, the ideas. Everything that was once part of your future, is now gone. And in the blink of an eye.

As horrible as it sounds, there were so many times I wished he would have died instead of leaving, because it hurts me so deeply to know that he was still living but choosing to do so without me. And that level of rejection, by the person I loved most in the world, damn near killed me.

There was no magic wand to take the pain away. I had to force myself to have patience to grieve, process, and heal. Which was SO much easier said than done. I still struggle with the rejection now, nearly five years later. It's a sting that I'm not sure will ever go away.

In the depths of my separation I struggled to find the right type of resources to help me through this special type of hell. The right kind of advice, coach, book, podcast, or blog that would meet me where I was during the confusing and shocking early stages of separation. Everything I came across was either a divorce busting method to get him to come back, sad separation stories with happy endings of reunion, or words of encouragement on the beauty life can be after divorce. No offense, but fuck that shit. When I was in the thick of it and I just needed something relatable to help me survive that emotional hell, I found nothing. Nothing that spoke to surviving the present moment, to get me through what was to come, or to help me learn to take care of myself in this fragile state.

I would have done anything to feel better. Just to numb the pain, distract my mind, and take me out of my reality for a bit. I read countless books, worked with a therapist, went on personal development retreats, traveled the world, spoiled myself, and maxed out credit cards through retail therapy. I don't regret any of it, and I was very fortunate to have had the finances and flexibility to do so.

For a long time I could not face the pain because it was just too much. Which is okay. Whatever journey you're on right now and the things you need to do to make yourself feel good is perfectly okay, no matter what anyone else says. Others don't get a say in your healing, even if they've been through a divorce or grieving situation themselves. There's no one-size-fits all method. The only one who has any say in your healing process is you. It's YOUR journey, no one else's.

My journey was long, and ridiculously hard. But even on the hardest days, when I was literally on my knees crying and screaming at the top of my lungs, praying for God to take the pain away, I knew in my heart that God gave me this experience and took me down this rocky road for a reason. There had to be a purpose for this pain. And I believe, perhaps a small part of it, was to share my experience with others as a way to help them down a similar path.

I started writing this book on December 07, 2019 in Aguas Caliente, Peru, one year, four months, 26 days after he told me he was leaving. I finished writing on September 6, 2023. Over five years since that dreadful day in July 2018 and it's been one hell of a journey to get here.

I hit rock bottom, and stayed there for a long time.

Today, I am better. I can feel joy and speak my truth, but I still have a hard time saying his name. Not a day goes by where I don't think about him, either from a state of love or hate or indifference. And he still haunts my dreams most nights. Divorce has been a big part of my life and story.

Enter With an Open Mind

Whatever your reason was for picking up this book, there are a few things you should know about before we get started.

The first is that I have strong faith in God. I will talk about how my faith helped me through this journey and I understand and respect that not everyone has the same beliefs. The strength my faith gave me during this time gave me the reassurance that I wasn't alone, that God had a bigger and better plan for me, and that this experience was teaching me a valuable lesson to carry me into my next chapter.

The second is that I believe in marriage and I do not believe in divorce. My marriage vows were the most important commitment I ever made. I did not give up on my marriage or the man throughout my entire year and a half separation. I didn't sign divorce papers. I could not let that be on my conscience by signing, to me that was giving up. So our divorce went through the court system as contested. I actually didn't even know I was officially divorced until the papers finally found their way to me three months after they were stamped by the judge.

The third thing I'd like you to know before reading, is that this book is not about my ex-husband. This is my story of a journey through separation and divorce. It is not to get back at him, defame him, or share any war stories. I know in my heart he is a good man, despite the hurt he caused me.

The final thing I'd like you to know is that we did not have children together. So I do not have the experience of that extra layer of complexity when children are involved.

Separation and divorce are extremely vulnerable and writing about them in the past has caused me additional heartbreak. My family has been embarrassed that I would speak so openly about something they deemed was too private to share. Old friends took what I was saying out of context and spread rumors around my hometown. The reaction and actions of supposed friends and family, combined with my own fears of sharing my personal experiences so vulnerably, has held me back for such a long time. But if my story, experiences, healing and recovery practices, and resources that I share could help just one person going through their own experience of separation, divorce, or any type of loss, then it will have all been worth it.

This is a book about resilience and moving through grief, so for anyone who is experiencing grief in any form this book will support you on your journey to finding self and wholeness even with a broken heart.

What to Expect From This Book

I start at the very beginning. When my separation was new, raw, and I was completely lost. The story and chapters build off of one another as you travel throughout this book as I moved from surviving to thriving and writing my next chapter of life post-divorce.

Drizzled throughout the chapters are my favorite quotes and mantras that were beacons of light that I now hold close to my heart. Within each chapter I share my journal entries and stories of my first couple of years of separation and divorce and the tools, resources, and practices that helped me through those times. These can also be found on my website at parableofabrokenheart.com/resources to easily refer to whenever you need.

My Gift To You

If you are here during your own separation and divorce, please know that as hard and impossible as it might seem right now, it will get better. Eventually. Grief is not linear. It's a roller coaster with ups, downs, twists, turns, and sudden drops coupled with the anxiety of not knowing what's coming next. Everyone heals at their own pace, so please, just give yourself grace.

Listen to what your body, mind, and soul need and give yourself that. If it's reasonable, of course. You can't rush this healing. Let it be and lean into it. Trust that you're being held and guided to make the best choices and decisions for yourself.

It is my hope that mine can be a story you can lean into for inspiration and strength if, or when, you need it.

This book is my gift to you. This is my story and my survival guide to the hell of separation and divorce. A compilation of the self-soothing tools and resources I learned and practiced to help me navigate the most challenging time of my life. This is a book to share my experiences in hopes that it helps you through your own hardships. To show you that healing is possible and that life goes on, even if it looks completely different than what you planned and imagined for yourself.

If you're like I was, I wanted answers and solutions *yesterday* to help me breathe, get through the next minute, hour, day.... Something tangible to put into action to help me just move forward.

Contained within this book is what worked to help me find **me** again. I hope it helps you on your journey too.

yes,
you will rise from the ashes,
but the burning comes first.

for this part,
darling,
you must be brave.

kalen dion

Chapter 1

The End

Mantra: *My story is my strength*

I married young. We started dating when I was 21 and the summer I turned 23 we tied the knot. My Bachelor's of Science with a degree in Biology went out the window when I moved back to my hometown after university to marry the man of my dreams. I started a part-time job at a bank to allow for the flexibility of our busy lifestyle of business travel for my husband's work. He treated me like a queen with flowers on monthly anniversaries, sweet love Post-it notes every morning, and the most thoughtful gifts after his long work trips away from home. He made me feel loved beyond what I ever imagined was possible and we had a beautiful life.

We built our dream home at our favorite place in the world, where we wanted our kids to grow up. It was close to family and it would be our home-base wherever life would take us. We became international "snowbirds" moving twice a year to and from our Canadian summer home to our Arizona winter condo. I woke up each morning incredibly grateful to be living my dream life, surrounded by so much love and beauty. We had been through a lot together in our six years of marriage, more trials and tribulations than I think a lot of couples do in their early years. I truly thought we could make it through anything.

Six months before he left we decided to start trying for a family.

I had devoted six years to being the best wife I could be. Our families were very traditional Eastern European farmers of the Christian faith, so I played the part of the perfect housewife that my mom and mother-in-law had set as an example—fully managing the household so everything was taken care of when my dear husband came home exhausted from work. He was the breadwinner of our family and traveled often for his work so I kept myself available and flexible so that whatever free time he had outside of business, we could spend it together.

We lived and we loved hard. We created the most beautiful memories I will never forget.

I (seemingly) had it all—multiple homes, luxury vehicles, extensive travel, the closets full of beautiful clothes, designer bags, and freedom from financial stress. I was completely taken care of, and he always made sure I felt protected.

But despite the glamorous lifestyle, I slowly started to fall into a deep depression. Which took a major toll on our marriage.

I felt like I had no purpose. I had a hard time finding a job while we lived in the United States, became extremely insecure about my body, developed an absurd case of social anxiety, had little control over my emotions, and didn't know how to communicate anything that was going on inside me. In our culture mental health didn't exist, you just sucked it up and tried harder. This inner turmoil went on for about two years, and things got tougher in our marriage. We drifted, had some really bad fights that left lasting wounds, and had a horrible marriage counselor that I believe made things worse (*kudos to me for hiring her twice*).

It was July and we had just said goodnight to some friends after hosting them for dinner in our home when he started the conversation. In just four words my world crumbled.

"I want a separation"

"You want a separation or a divorce?" I replied.

"What's the difference?"

I paced around our kitchen in shock, crying hard. He sat at the island, cool as a cucumber as he sipped on a scotch on the rocks.

We stayed up for the next four or five hours spinning the conversation in circles. He slept in the spare bedroom and I went to sleep in there with him.

The next day we revisited the conversation over and over and over again but by that evening, it was like nothing ever happened. We did our classic "sweep it under the rug" style that followed most disagreements. We hung out and watched TV together—a series we had been watching on Netflix the last couple weeks. We took the dogs out for a long walk around our neighborhood. He was leaving the next day to head back down south for work. I helped him pack. He said he would be back in a month or so, at the end of the summer.

He slept in our bed that night.

I helped wake him up early the next day to drive early to the airport. We kissed goodbye. He asked that I not call or text him for the next couple of days. He needed time to think.

That was the last time we shared a bed. The last time I hugged him. The last time I kissed his lips.

I had so much hope. I believed we could get through this. We had been through so much together already, we could get through anything.

The next couple weeks I threw myself into whatever I could—books, marriage coaching programs, therapy, advisement and prayers from our priest. Anything to try to fix what was happening in my marriage. To fix us. This could not be happening. It simply could not be happening.

He asked if we could talk. It was a Sunday afternoon and one week before our sixth wedding anniversary.

This call was raw. It was a month after he left and we had barely talked since he'd been away. He told me he needed space, and I respected that. But I was under the impression he would still be coming home and I had the highest hopes that in the last month of being separated he would change his mind. That he missed me and we could fix this.

When I picked up the phone, he was angry. So, so angry.

We screamed back and forth for more than two hours. I bawled my eyes out. I vividly remember pacing around our house walking in line with the hardwood flooring. I was focussing so hard on keeping within those straight lines, the only thing I had control over at that moment.

I don't remember much of the specifics. Whenever we fought it was like my mind would shut down, an unconscious coping mechanism I later learned from my therapist. I just remember that he was furious and done with me. He said he didn't even love me anymore. A month ago he said he wasn't in love with me, but would always love me. Now there was no more love left.

I was the problem. **I** was why he was leaving. **I** wasn't good enough, and I felt like I was being thrown out like trash.

After talking in circles for hours my body and mind was exhausted, and I knew he meant every word.

When we hung up, I went into panic mode. My life had officially just fallen apart.

Up to that point I had only told my mom and two close friends what was happening. No one else knew. Not even his family who I was still spending a lot of time with, as they just lived down the street from us. I called our best friends, a couple, that were our closest friends throughout our entire relationship. Someone needed to talk some sense into him. This wasn't right. This couldn't be happening. It hit me like a semi-trailer full of bricks that it was all real.

Our friends were in shock. They knew we had been having troubles the past year, but they visited us a week before he left and commented on how good we seemed to be doing. When I got off the phone with our friends telling them the news, they called my husband. When they called me back to tell me what happened they confirmed that he seemed to have made up his mind and there was no changing it.

I called my mom. I couldn't be alone. She came over and took care of me.

A lot happened that next week...

The panic attacks started that night. I would cry so hard I couldn't breathe and would circle into a panicked frenzy. The following weeks I would have panic attacks multiple times a day. Another close friend, who was in her general practitioner residency, suggested I go see my family doctor and get something to help me cope. Never before had I considered my mental health, but during that visit the doctor helped me unpack years and years of depression-related behaviors and tendencies. I was diagnosed with clinical depression, started on medication for depression and the panic attacks, and... put on suicide watch. The local health practitioner would call me daily for two weeks to make sure I was safe and okay. If you're familiar with antidepressants it takes up to six weeks before you start getting the benefits, so I continued to fall into a deep, deep depression. I had zero will to live.

I began to disintegrate. I couldn't look after myself. I didn't eat. I couldn't sleep. I couldn't function let alone work. I was doing free-lance work remotely, and had just been promoted to management with the agency I was with. I had to email them to say I would be out the next two weeks due to a family emergency.

This was an emergency. My family had just completely fallen apart.

My best friend came to relieve my mom and even though she had three young kids at home and their farm had just started their harvest, she stayed with me. The truest act of friendship I've ever experienced.

Within two months I had lost 30 pounds. My hormones were so messed up from extreme adrenal fatigue and most days I couldn't get out of bed.

The story doesn't get better for a long, long time. For nearly nine months I physically, mentally, and emotionally could not do anything. Grief had completely taken over every molecule in my body.

Where we lived in Canada a couple needs to be separated for a full year before filing for divorce. So in the back of my mind there was still hope. Still hope that he would realize what he was giving up and come back to me. So I never gave up, even though there might have only been a 0.25% chance of him changing his mind, I was going to wait. Because I was his wife and I wasn't going to give up on him.

That whole year it felt like my life was in limbo. Waiting. Hoping. Praying.

I didn't get my fairytale ending. He didn't come back to me on a gleaming white horse where everything was magically forgiven. It wasn't until mid-January 2020, over a year and a half later, that I learned that I was officially divorced. The paperwork had been signed and dated by the judge three months earlier at the beginning of November. And while I didn't get a fairytale ending, my story does have a happy ending. Not the happy ending I envisioned, but happy all the same.

My journey was so hard and lonely that it felt impossible at times. I remember when a friend said to me in the early days "One year from now things will be so different." So I held on to that one year mark. This pain is just temporary. One year was enough time for change—when I would know if he was coming back or not, when I would have made some plans for my new future, when I could maybe finally breathe again. I focused on just getting through another day. **If my life could be turned upside down in a second, my world could look completely different in a year.** I moved forward and grew that next year, two years, and am still using the tools I learned. I had no other choice. I found happiness in finding myself again, becoming my own person, finding my purpose and passion. I found happiness in embracing this new solo chapter of my life and getting to know myself again. What I liked, what I disliked, what I was capable of. I found my independence. I found me.

God never said "Understand Me."
He said, "*Trust Me.*"

Chapter 2

Alone

Mantra: *I am strong*

I had a trip planned with my brother to the Canadian Rocky Mountains, which just happened to be two weeks after that devastating phone call when I knew he wasn't coming home. After my best friend left to get back to her family I realized I couldn't be alone, and kept the trip despite the horrible timing.

I begged my doctor to give me emotional support dog permissions so I could travel with my little dog, Finn. He was by my side 24/7, my living, breathing security blanket and true therapy dog in those first impossible months. I didn't know how I was going to survive without having him with me on the trip. Apparently though I wasn't too far gone, even while on suicide watch, to get a letter for plane access so take him with me.

My brother picked me up at the airport with a weighted blanket and stuffed animal I had requested. I remember us driving into the Rockies, me in the passenger seat of his yellow Chevy Cobalt, the car I got for my 17th birthday that was passed down to him. It was the end of summer and still quite warm out but I was having full-body shakes, freezing as I was buried underneath the weighted blanket and two other blankets, holding on to that stuffed animal for dear life. The look in his eyes as I explained what was going on is a look I will never forget. As the older sibling I was the one always protecting him. I've never seen him so concerned for me. He took such good care of me that weekend as we explored the mountains and I attempted to enjoy the trip with him.

I rejiggered my flights and carried on to Arizona to go see my husband afterwards. We needed to see each other face-to-face.

He refused to let me stay at our place, and he got me an Airbnb down the road. I had already been completely moved out of our condo. There was not a trace of my existence left in that place. His wedding ring was already off.

I stayed for a week. That was the first time I felt truly alone. There was no one checking in on me, no one to assure me or calm me down. No mom, no dogs, no friends. Just me.

I vividly remember falling to my knees multiple times that week. Crying out so loudly to God, begging him to take the pain away. Nothing could ever compare to the pain I felt inside. Uncontrollable sobbing, every piece of me hurt, and it never ceased. This was a pain I had to learn to live with, and it was only just the beginning.

That trip I met up with my girlfriends, all of which were the wives of our couple group we had become close with. I had lost 15 pounds in the last six weeks on my already thin frame and everyone was commenting on how good I looked—until they learned the reason why. Sharing the raw and real of what is going on in our lives was so freeing. I needed people in my corner after being abandoned and rejected. I needed their hugs, supportive words, and honestly, just time to speak freely and openly.

Looking back at the pictures from that trip, I barely recognize myself. I was smiling in group pictures, but my eyes were empty like there was no one inside.

I had gone from living with my parents as a teenager, to the dorms with a roommate in university, and straight into moving in with him after graduation to live out our happily ever after. So I had truly never been alone as an adult. This was a first and it scared the crap out of me.

The self-help books I read, Instagram profiles I followed, TikTok videos I watched, and my therapist helped me learn that I had zero self-love. And after that realization came the one when I realized how ass-backwards I had been raised to see myself and my marriage.

"You need to love yourself before others."

"You need to be whole, and be a whole person in your relationship"

"We're all individuals experiencing life together."

Umm, what? This was news to me.

This was the total opposite of what I was raised to believe and knew marriage to be.

To me, marriage was two becoming one (*cue the Spice Girls' song*). Sharing life, love, and memories. Building and growing together as one. Marrying so young I never grew into being my own person, I fell hard in love to being "an everything" for someone else. So now that I was alone—I was *alone* alone, and didn't know how to handle it. Being alone was a first for me at 29 years old.

I came across a TED Talk by my now favorite poet, Najwa Zebian (*which is linked in the online resources at parableofabrokenheart.-com/resources*) and it resonated with exactly what I was experiencing:

I had no home and with that I was content, because I never knew what it felt like to feel like home. So you built a home for me, and all of my scattered pieces suddenly came together. Somewhere, I put my heart to sleep as you cradled my worries away.

I woke up one day cold, abandoned, without a roof on top, without windows or walls, without you. And you wonder why I am so unable to let you go.

Before you, I never knew what a home was. You gave me a taste of heaven, and with your hands you took it away. Once you enter heaven, you can never live again the same way.

najwa zebian

I have always taken the word "home" so seriously. I've heard people use the word to refer to any place where they rest their head at night —a hotel room, or a friend's place while on vacation. Home was always a special place to me, so I don't use it lightly. Home was my parents' farm, so when I went away to university I never called my dorm or campus apartments home. And when we married, home became where we lived, despite our many moves, and eventually our dream house at the lake. No matter where we were in the world or during our time down in Arizona, our condo was our condo and home was our lake house back in Canada, near where we both had grown up. The place that had so much meaning to us as a couple and family. So Nejwa's words really hit hard using the home analogy. There is no place like home.

He was my home. I built my home in him and my self-worth became directly correlated to how much value and attention he put on that "home." My self-love was so nonexistent during our marriage I couldn't even understand how or why this incredible man loved me. I had no concept of what self-love even meant. I didn't love myself and my value was based on his love for me. And because he loved me, I was special. So when he left I became homeless and empty.

It was terrifying. My whole world—my home—disappeared and I had no one to lean on. So despite my resistance, if I wanted to survive I had no other choice but to learn to lean on myself.

Many of my decisions—after severely struggling to first of all to even trust myself to make decisions—over the next couple years were based on my aloneness. Where I lived, because I couldn't live somewhere with snow and not have someone waiting for me at home or to call if I got stuck in a storm or snowbank, so I moved to the only place in Canada that didn't snow. I had to live somewhere I felt safe and secure, so I moved into a gated community. I needed a newer vehicle because I was terrified of an expensive breakdown that I wouldn't know how to fix. I was afraid of the maintenance costs of owning a home like replacing shingles or a broken down furnace. I was afraid of a single-income household and managing my finances for the first time as an adult, so I eventually sold my house and moved into a rental.

I lived in so much fear of being alone. And then aloneness became my best friend, and being around people exhausted me. Because I didn't know how to be happy it exhausted me to have to pretend when around others. *Hello depression.*

After our separation was formalized, I moved down to Arizona, away from my family and closest friends to be closer to him, in case he changed his mind and wanted to come back home to me and our dogs. I had a couple of very close friends in Arizona so I wasn't completely alone or starting new in an unfamiliar place.

I rented a big, brand new, modern four bedroom house that was way out of my budget, because I refused to downgrade my lifestyle because of him leaving and it's hard finding a rental with three dogs. That big rental house became my sanctuary for the next year. That house held me, heard my cries, my prayers, and helped me start to build my own home.

I had a great therapist back in Saskatchewan, and we tried to carry on our sessions virtually when I moved away but they just weren't the same. So despite still being very mentally unstable, I went without a therapist for a couple months (*Not a good idea FYI—when you find a good one, don't let them go!*). Instead I hired a transformational life coach, someone who could help me navigate this major life transition with easy to implement action plans and practices.

Ava was a godsend, and I know she was divinely put in my life to help me during this time. She was exactly what I needed when I needed her. She was like my paid best friend so I could stop being such a dark cloud over my precious relationships. I ended up working with her for six months, and the first month was really just creating a foundation to stand on again.

To help me work through my feelings of loneliness, Ava gave me some incredible tools that I still use today.

1. Get a massage or massage yourself

I've always been a huge fan of bodywork, and would get regular massages for muscle therapy reasons but there was another piece I never considered or needed before. The power behind feeling another person's touch.

2. Take baths

Water is the only element that holds us. It's actually like a warm hug. Part of water's soothing nature is being encapsulated in warmth, other than our own. Whenever I was feeling overwhelmed, anxious, or alone, I would take a bath. Bathing grew into a ritual and an almost ceremonial practice by dimming the lights, lighting a candle, adding in nurturing essential oils and epsom salts, flower petals and putting on a face mask. Such a simple and easy thing to help soothe my body and soul.

3. Lean on your faith or spirituality

My faith grew in leaps and bounds during this time because I needed a relationship with God now more than ever. Initially, this was for selfish reasons only—to remind myself that I wasn't truly alone, a reliance on his omnipresence and assurance by his word.

I grew up in the Lutheran faith, but we married Catholic, his religion. To me, it's all the same God and the type of church didn't matter. When he left, I went to seek counsel from our priest, who also became a family friend over the years. He gave me a customized set of novena prayers for strength and guidance. Novena prayers are two different daily bible verses to pray upon for nine days (available at parableofabrokenheart.com/resources).

I repeated these prayers, morning and night, like my life depended on it. Which it kind of did. I wanted the power of God's word and my dedication to the novena prayers to bring him back, more than anything. The more I prayed, being the good and dedicated Christian girl I thought I should be, and the closer to God I became, I believed it would make a difference and God would answer my prayers.

No such luck as God would have it, despite the countless rounds of the novena prayers. But just as the priest had intended, each passage held an important message that he wanted me to hear. I clung to these words for comfort and reassurance. One passage in particular became my mantra:

> "God is within her, she will not fall" – Psalm 46:5

And I would lean into God's strength within me to keep me going.

In my faith I learned to surrender and fall completely into trusting God's greater plan for me. I knew there had to be more than this—I had to be experiencing this pain and suffering for a greater reason. Surrendering is hard, especially for a self-proclaimed control freak like myself, so this level of surrendering didn't happen right away and I'm still constantly reminding myself to have reckless faith. Leaning into the idea that I was having this experience for a reason was a key component in my healing journey. Letting go of the control, surrendering, and trusting that this is all happening for me, instead of to me.

Another prayer that was introduced to me in the early days was the Prayer of Surrender:

> *"Dear God,*
>
> *Being of Light, I surrender this relationship to you. Take it, please. Help me to know what to do. Give me the strength and courage to do it. Help me to remember I am not in charge. Help me to be loving and kind. Help me to be of service. Help me to be who You would have me be. Help me to remember that whatever You have in store for me must, by definition, be greater than what I can imagine for myself. Thank you."*

This prayer, in addition to my novena prayers and routine morning and evening prayers, was pivotal. The Prayer of Surrender reminded me that I wasn't in control and the idea that whatever God had in store for me would be so much greater beyond any plan or dream I had was freeing. It reminded me to rest and let Him take care of me. That I would be okay.

to all of the lights who chose
to dim when I was in the
darkness, thank you for
teaching me that
my own light is all I need

najwa zebian

Chapter 3

Time and Space to Heal

Mantra: *This too shall pass*

They say time heals all wounds, but I don't quite agree with that statement. In my experience I've just learned how to live with the pain, the pain doesn't lessen. It's been five years since he left as I'm finalizing this book and reliving what I went through still stings me to the core. I still get angry and sad—the whole roller coaster of emotions. Some moments it even takes my breath away how much it still hurts. The only difference is I've learned to live with these feelings, the pain is still very real.

If anything, time is our biggest enemy during difficult life transitions. It moves too slow. We want so badly to move past the pain as quickly as possible.

What we go through when separating and divorcing is life-altering. It isn't something that just goes away or that we can simply move on from after a few months. It is a major life transition, regardless of how common it has become. And for anyone who has had a different experience, I really envy you.

Don't let anyone tell you how you should feel or what your healing timeline should be.

Don't compare yourself to others' stories.

Do what you need to do for you, for your mind, body, and soul.

The first month after he left I only told three people, and that month was solely focused on getting him back. The second month, when I realized he wasn't coming back I told a couple more sets of friends. But it wasn't until three months after he left when I told my family and would cautiously talk to others about it who asked.

He was upset that I didn't make it public right away and waited so long to tell my people. But he no longer had any say in what I shared or didn't. This was my story now, not ours, and I had to take it at my own pace. It took me a long time to be able to verbalize what was going on without crumbling. In some ways I maybe wasn't accepting this new reality by not sharing it, but also it was no one's business either.

Give yourself whatever you need, and as much as possible.

Judging ourselves will be inevitable. We blame, replay memories, play the woulda-shoulda-coulda game in our minds over and over. We get upset with ourselves when we do great one day and the next day is an absolute dumpster fire shit show. Healing is NOT linear, it's the worst, most nauseating, roller coaster ride.

Just take it day by day. Every day will be different. Take it as it comes with no judgment. These are some practices that helped me ease into my new reality and take care of myself.

1) Listen to what you need, emotionally, physically, and spiritually.

Ask yourself what you need that day and give to yourself whatever it is you need. (Within reason, of course I can only go to Lululemon so many times in a month).

I try to give myself one free day a week where I lean into what my body and soul really needs. Sometimes it looks like laying on the couch all day, others it might be going on an impromptu road trip, or taking the dogs for a hike. Give yourself grace, you're only human and we need rest in various forms sometimes.

2) Create some normalcy for yourself.

My coach, Ava, that I hired during my separation, introduced this extremely simple, common sense practice. Life is chaotic and all over the place. Your world has just been turned upside down but you can still gift yourself a replenishing and nourishing morning and evening routine that doesn't waver. Mornings were tough for me because I couldn't sleep for the first two-plus years, but I was a rockstar at my evening routine. It looked something like this:

- Put on pajamas
- Brush teeth, floss, and put in retainer
- Wash face. Cleanse, tone, serum, and overnight cream (*my skin was perfection during my separation*). Add on lash growth serum
- Crawl into bed
- Lights out
- Say prayers and gratitudes from the day
- Breathwork, either box breathing (Inhale for four seconds, hold for four, exhale for four, hold again for four. Then repeat 10 times.) or just 10 deep, slow breaths.

Super basic right? I had control over this small piece of my day, and I relished in this accomplishment of doing one thing right every day even if it was the most fundamental form of hygiene and self-care.

3) Move negative energy.

Don't rush anything, including negative emotions. These too need to be processed and the negative energy needs to be released from our bodies. I held on to everything for so long the pain almost became addictive, because it was now a part of my identity. Hormone imbalances, extreme adrenal fatigue, dramatic weight loss followed by dramatic weight gain, insomnia, constant fatigue... just a few of the fun things I dealt with. The anger was the worst.

For me, the anger turned into a physical response. First hit was nausea. A lump grew in the back of my throat that instantly made me nauseous. Then it turned into rage. I would get so angry, I would want to take a bat and beat the shit out of a punching bag to release this frustration. Repeated thoughts of how the F did I get here, how is this my life, I just want to go home... These thoughts would come at me over and over again and it would create so much anger and rage within my body. I was physically holding on to so much of it for so long, it needed a release.

I never did get a bat or a punching bag, it seemed a little expensive and dramatic, but here some things that helped me move through and release the anger and rage:

Move the energy through movement

A long walk, yoga, sweat session at the gym, laps in the pool, etc. Move your body to move out those emotions.

Move the energy through physical releases

Hitting a pillow, boxing, or trying out a rage room where you can pay to break shit and people clean up your mess afterwards!

Move the energy through verbal releases

If you are like me, I often don't speak up or defend myself when I should. I get too emotional, even in the smallest confrontations. I've learned that we need to exercise our voices to free ourselves from all of those thoughts that have been ruminating over-and-over in our minds. Go out into the forest, a field, or somewhere people won't think you're crazy and just let it out. Scream, yell, hoot, holler, scream-cry, or burst out in absolute disbelief fit of laughter. Make noise. Move that shit out. And if you don't have a quiet or private spot, a thick pillow always works.

Emotional Freedom Technique (EFT)/Tapping

Tapping has proved to be a powerful releasing technique in my practice where you literally tap different areas of your body while saying some self-loving affirmations. If you've never heard of or experienced tapping before I've provided a diagram, thorough outline, YouTube link and some of my favorite prompts at parableofabrokenheart.com/resources for you to try.

4) Cord-Cutting Meditation

In a very literal sense, cord-cutting meditations are a form of guided meditations where we envision breaking a physical connection, a cord, resembling an attachment to something or someone. I've done different versions of cord-cutting meditations with different facilitators, all are relatively the same. You are guided to imagine the cord between yourself and the person, emotion, or situation that's weighing on you. This cord can be whatever material your mind projects, natural fibers, metal, nylon... The facilitator will lead you through cutting that cord, symbolizing detachment—it no longer being a part of you.

I've done cord-cutting meditations dozens of times now and each time I feel a little bit more detached and free. *Who knew you could have so many cords attached to the same thing?* Cord-cutting reminded me I was my own entity, I had control over what outside situations had influence over me, and those negative pieces weighing me down could no longer anchor in me.

Time and space are both relative, as is your healing journey. What you need at this point of time will be different from any other trial or tribulation you've experienced. This is new territory you're exploring, be gentle yourself as you learn to adapt.

be patient

you cannot remove a person
from your bones while your
hands are still shaking

l.e. bowman

Chapter 4

Quick Happiness Fixes

Mantra: *I am always in choice*

Distraction became my best coping mechanism in the early days of my separation—and by early days I actually mean the first year and a half.

I wasn't out partying, dating, doing drugs. I isolated myself, strictly consumed protein shakes, toast, and takeout, and took sleeping pills just to fall asleep each night.

The first 18 months of the separation I traveled to five countries, four provinces, seven states, more than 16 different destinations, and did an international move from Arizona back to Canada.

I recall catching up with a friend during that time, and after asking how I was doing I made a joke that all I was doing was "running" and she said, "Oh good for you, running is so healthy." To which I replied and corrected her that I was running from my feelings.

When I wasn't on a plane traveling to be with friends, family, or just on a solo trip, you could probably find me on my couch for 12 plus hours a day or in bed. Naps became a necessity as I was constantly exhausted, and I could count on one hand the number of times I actually worked from my desk in my home office that year.

I was in a deep depression, and at the time, I didn't think I wanted out. The only thing I wanted—other than my husband to come home —was to not feel. I wanted an escape from my unbearable reality.

I couldn't sleep, I barely ate, I struggled to focus at work, and I became a huge dark cloud of negative energy with my friends. But, when I was out of my house and taking breaks from my reality I could actually pull off a smile and pretend I was powering through like a champ.

The little things really made a difference to help me get through the days, and my biggest hack was training my brain to refocus my negative thoughts into something different, something positive. Yes, this was a different way of "running" and not working through my feelings, but when you're living DEEP in the grief it's okay to give yourself some grace and a mental break from your reality.

These were some of my quick happiness fixes that I found most helpful to refocus towards something positive, and rarely, put a genuine smile on my face.

1: Create a "Happy Box"

In my world, Christmas 2018, the first holiday season alone, didn't happen. I asked my cousin to come with me to Mexico over Christmas and New Years to avoid the holidays. As I spent my days beach-side, inhaling as much tequila as possible followed by a strong sleeping pill before bed every night, my mind was still drowned in sadness, even in paradise. I don't know where this idea came from, but sometime during those 10 days in Playa del Carmen I came up with my "Happy Box."

A Happy Box is an imaginary box that I pictured in the back of my mind where I would store two to three things that made me smile, giggle, or ignite some glimmer of hope. This box looked like a plain cardboard box that opened on the top, with a big yellow smiley face on the front.

Whenever a bad, sad, or negative thought would come to mind I would quickly go to my Happy Box and recite the memories I put in there. My horrible short term memory would usually do the trick too by spending more time thinking of what I put in the box versus reliving those memories, extending the distraction time.

While in Mexico, I would have breakfast every morning at the resort's all-inclusive buffet and eat outside at the same table in the corner that gave me a really good people-watching view. Most mornings a multi-generational Italian family would have breakfast around the same time, just a couple tables over. There were two small children in the group, a boy and girl, cousins I think. These kids were so entertaining, and I equally enjoyed watching their luxuriously dressed parents and grandparents reactions to their silliness. These kids fuelled my Happy Box.

One morning, as the family was finishing up breakfast and exiting the outdoor patio to go back into the main restaurant, the little girl used her "special powers" to open up the automatic doors. She took a big jump in front of the doors and raised her arms overhead. And *magically* the doors would slide open and she would giggle with glee. The look of pure fascination and smugness of having successfully completed this magic trick gave me so much joy, I put that right into the Happy Box and visited that moment frequently the rest of the trip.

A different day, the father of that beautiful Italian family strolled into the patio to join the rest of his family carrying the young boy, who was wearing a neck gaiter over his head, covering his face with just a small tuft of hair peeking out the top. To make it even better, the neck gaiter was covered in dinosaur print. Freaking hilarious, especially since the father had a completely blank look on his face, appearing to have just had the struggle of his life getting this little boy down to breakfast. Priceless. That went directly into the Happy Box, too, for future enjoyment and a quick happiness fix.

The memories we put in our Happy Boxes don't have to be anything elaborate. You don't have to go out looking for what to put in your Happy Box, it could be something from the past or even just the thought of someone or something you love. Anytime you think of your current situation and it brings you down into a spiral of negativity, switch your thoughts to your Happy Box. I promise you, it'll work everytime. Even if it brings you the smallest smirk or gives your brain a five second break from the sadness, it will have worked its own special magic as a quick happiness fix.

2: Animal Therapy

If you aren't a fan of animals, maybe skip this one. I have three dogs, and while I don't suggest a commitment as large as your own pack, borrowing a friend's animal for a quick pet or stopping one on the street can do the trick.

My pups are the light of my life. My only constant over the last 12 years. They are the truest form of unconditional love I have ever experienced and when I am with them it is guaranteed they will bring a smile to my face. Even when I could barely look after myself and their care took a major backseat—when I didn't walk them for months and we lived very boring lives inside during the blistering Arizona summer heat, they were my constant companions and always happy. They would lick away my tears and were by my side whenever I needed them. It was a major transition for all of us. Having them to take care of, even when I didn't do a good job of it, kept me going. I needed them and they needed me. Without them, I don't know how I would have survived.

3: Spend Time Outside

I've always loved living on the outskirts of a city or town and the forest is so healing and rejuvenating for me. Connecting with nature helps me remember that my problems are so small in the grand scheme of life, and how beautiful life can be. Whenever I'm in a rut or just need a break, I go to the forest or edge of the water and just sit. Soaking in and being present with the force of life around me brings me peace.

4: TikTok/Feel Good Videos, Quotes, or Reels

Okay, hear me out. It's not all pre-teens dancing, I've learned a LOT on TikTok. I've heard some of my new favorite quotes and speaker clips, and my algorithm has definitely shifted towards showing some of the most unbelievably ridiculous and silly content out there. Which makes me very happy. My best friend, her husband, and I have a group chat where we share TikToks. So yes, I am a TikTok fan because it makes me happy. Simple as that. And watching TikTok videos for 10-15 minutes before bed each night brings me so much joy, that it has become a quick happiness fix for me. I love ending the day with laughter and going to bed happy. So whether it's TikTok, Instagram, YouTube,or sharing memes with a friend, find some feel-good videos to enjoy each day.

5: Plan Something to Look Forward To

As I mentioned, I did a LOT of traveling during my separation and this served as the ultimate distraction in planning and execution of a trip. But it doesn't have to be something big and extravagant to look forward to. It could simply be scheduling a hike in your calendar, or a coffee date with a friend. Treating yourself to a massage or going to a movie. Anything that is outside your norm and brings you excitement to think about. Dream about a bucket list trip, about finding the next love of your life, dream about something that lights your soul on fire. Look forward to the future. Looking forward to something for yourself, anything, no matter how small, is a great happiness fix.

these mountains that you are
carrying, you were only
supposed to climb

najwa zebian

Chapter 5

Simple Reminders

Mantra: *I am enough*

The first three to four months of separation I would call my best friend most nights before bed in a panicked frenzy to get her assurance that I would get through this alive. She is seriously an angel, even while wrangling her own kids through their bedtime routine she always answered my call and would help calm me down. Throughout the day I created constant reminders of reassurance and empowering affirmations that I would plant either on myself or around my home. At first they were a need, then they turned into practices of self-love.

Just like quick happiness fixes, these simple reminders carried me through some of my darkest moments. These are some of my favorite practices that I still use today.

1: Mirror Sticky Notes

Mirror talk is real talk people. As I talk about in the Reality Pause chapter, I remember the first time I ever stood in front of a mirror and told myself, "I loved you."

There is seriously nothing more powerful that seeing and hearing yourself say the words you need to hear the most. Even if you don't believe the words at the time, this act of self-love is POWERFUL.

So I dare you, walk up to a mirror right now, look yourself straight in the eye and say, "I love you."

How did that feel? Did you try to look away? Did you cry? Was it uncomfortable? Did you see your five year old self looking back at you in need of a hug. **You** can give yourself all the love you need. This is a great reminder that we don't need these affirmations from others, we can give them to ourselves.

My bathroom mirror was covered in sticky notes. These notes also creeped over to my full length mirror in my bedroom at one point. They ended up being a beautiful collage of affirmations, mantras, Bible verses, song lyrics, and my favorite quotes. Color coordinated in different Post-it note colors and marker combinations.

Reciting some, if not all, depending on what I needed that day, became a part of my daily routine. Here are some of my favorites. Do me a favor and as you read through these say them out loud and fully feel the words:

- I am worthy of love
- I am strong
- I create my own happiness and joy
- I am enough
- I rise above
- I can do hard things
- I am too strong to crumble (credit to my favorite pilates instructor for this one)
- God is within her, she will not fall - Psalm 46:5
- Hand it over to God
- Don't give up right before the miracle

- The Lord is close to the brokenhearted and saves those who are crushed in spirit. - Psalm 34:18

If you'd like inspiration for more, borrow the chapter mantras and start your own mirror sticky note collage.

2: Stuff Your Bra

NOT in the teenage way to instantly grow a couple extra cups, but if you haven't used your bra as a pocket before, welcome to the most secret of sacred places to keep special items or reminders close.

It is kind of like a security blanket to have a symbolic item on you as you go out to face the world, especially when you really don't want to. I started this ritual a couple months after he left. At first it was a small piece of red rock from Sedona, Arizona. A reminder of the powerful retreat I went on. Then I carried both the rock and a small turtle—a symbol one of my therapists introduced to me to represent perseverance and a reminder to take one step at a time. Like in the story of the turtle and the hare, "slow and steady wins the race," a turtle always wins and gets to its destination at its own pace. Even though it takes its time, it is always moving forward.

The days I forgot to take my rock and turtle along with me, I felt naked. They began to feel like my secret weapon and helped me get through the days.

I don't recommend anything too large or oddly shaped, for obvious reasons. It simply has to have some form of positive or hope-filled meaning to you. And if you can't immediately think of something, don't panic or rush—these things will often find you.

3: Your Sign

One of my practitioners introduced me to Gabby Bernstein and her book *The Universe Has Your Back*. In this masterpiece Gabby writes a whole chapter on choosing your sign and the power behind seeing this simple reminder. This rocked my world when I discovered this hack.

Above all, I believe in love. I love love. This did not change or waiver by everything that happened to me in my separation and divorce. In the months after he left, I was desperate to fill that void of love that he once consumed. I redirected this into looking for love in anything and everything around me which I saw come to me in the form of *hearts*. Suddenly I was seeing heart shapes everywhere. In rocks, clouds, leaves, on coasters at the coffee shops. I know it is a common shape, but I used the heart shape (even if it wasn't perfectly uniform) as a sign or simple reminder that I was going to be okay. That God was sending me love in all the places and that love still existed in the cruel chapter I was living through.

What's your sign? Mine has changed a bit over the years, depending on what I'm asking guidance for or what I need, but anytime I catch a glimpse of a heart, I know I am loved.

4: Home Decor Reminders

I am a huge advocate for making your home your sanctuary. For me, this has evolved to include reminders all around me that with just a glance at them or taking the time to appreciate their significance, I feel grounded.

I went through a phase where I LOVED farmhouse signs and had a couple custom made with quotes on them that served as daily simple reminders. One that I keep in my office is a Bible verse I've mentioned a couple times so far, "God is within her, she will not fall," Psalm 46:5. The other is in my bathroom so I see it every morning and night that says, "Let whatever you do today be enough," which I interpret as a reminder to give myself more grace. I've found a couple smaller desktop or tabletop decor pieces with my other favorite quotes that are scattered throughout my house. They are typically inexpensive decor pieces that always find me when I need their message the most.

Like a typical millennial, I am also guilty for looking at my phone way too much. So I've turned this into a practice of self-love by having affirmation apps as widgets on my home screen or push notifications from personal development apps set at different times of the day that give me a little dose of encouragement everytime I see them.

You might find yourself in a constant mode of self-criticism right now and being surrounded by affirmations like these (and the sticky notes) can help get you out of a funk—or just leave you a little better than they found you.

5: Proof of Magic

The proof of magic practice was introduced to me on a podcast I was listening to years ago, and ever since I have an ongoing list on my phone of good things that have happened to me. My list includes fond memories, synchronicities of one good thing snowballing into another over time, or things that I just write down in the moment as they happen. This list is, in the very literal sense, proof that magic is all around me. That good things happen and I am deserving of them all.

Some things on my list are:

- Hiring Ava as a yoga practitioner for my ladies forum weekend retreat and eventually hiring her as my transformational life coach, going to her retreat in Costa Rica which was an experience of a life-time.
- Creating a vision board with a picture of Machu Picchu and then being invited to go on a retreat in Peru two weeks later.
- Moving to my rental in Arizona and becoming best friends with my neighbor, Anna, who brought so much light into my life during that dark period of my separation.

- Manifesting the perfect home in Victoria.

Whether these experiences come to me by total coincidence, divine timing, or gifts of radical faith, they are good and reminiscing on them makes me feel good. So write your good, happy and magical things down. Even the little things. What good happened today?

6: Tattoo

I remember driving down highway 179 in Arizona heading into Sedona. I went to escape there for the extra long American Thanksgiving holiday weekend to hike through the healing red rocks with the dogs. Even though we were Canadian, we celebrated Thanksgiving in the US every year during our marriage. This was my first holiday alone (I spent the Canadian Thanksgiving at a retreat) and was feeling extra tender.

At this point I was exclusively listening to christian worship music on the K-Love radio station. You don't realize how many hit list songs are about either love or heartbreak until you're at rock bottom. The music played on other radio stations was actually a huge trigger for me. In part of strengthening my faith and avoiding my triggers, I found modern worship music really uplifting and calming.

As I was driving down the curvy and uber gorgeous highway 179, "Thy Will" by Hillary Scott & The Scott Family came over the radio. I instantly downloaded it on my phone and listened to it over and over and over. It was the message and reminder I needed in that tender moment that even though nothing was making sense, God had a bigger plan beyond the painful present.

In the Village of Oak Creek, just outside of Sedona, I drove past a tattoo shop that caught my eye. In addition to the Sedona red rock I'd been keeping in my bra for months, I wanted another reminder that I was not alone and that "Thy Will Be Done" as Hillary sings in the song and God tells us in the Lord's Prayer. So the next day I called the tattoo shop, and booked in for a session. This particular shop offered red dirt vortex tattoos, where they extracted the pigments from red dirt at the vortex sites around Sedona. Vortexes are a part of Sedona's draw, which are described to be a unique geological and spiritual phenomenon in the form of a swirling center of energy that produces spiritual, emotional, and physical effects. Sedona had become a very special place for me to come to heal, and nothing felt more fitting than to get a cross tattoo from the Boynton Canyon Vortex (Explained in the Reality Pause chapter) on my inner left wrist.

Now every time I look at this tattoo it is a reminder of so many things:

- My faith in a loving God.
- That I am never alone.
- My time among the beautiful red rocks in Sedona.
- And, that God's plan for me is better than anything I could ever imagine for myself, and the best is yet to come.

if you have to miss him,
miss him while you move.
while you walk
while you run.
toward, toward, toward.
miss him while you move on.
while you try.
while you dream.
don't stand still, never stand still.
don't wait, never wait.
live, live, live.
live without him.
it's okay to miss him.
but if you stand still while you do it,
it will bury you.

kristina mahr

Chapter 6

Hiring Your Besties

Mantra: *I am loved*

I was back home in Canada, about 10 months into my separation, visiting family and one of them said to me that I needed to stop wasting money on therapists and coaches and just get over it already.

Great advice, thank you for your loving support.

It's funny when moments like that happen, you instantly put up walls with certain people and I have never been able to be myself or open up around that person again. Because if I hadn't hired therapists, counselors, life coaches, and gone on retreats, I would have continued to be the darkest grey cloud hovering over my friendships, dragging down everyone around me that I loved.

My best friend is a Godsend. I honestly don't know how I would have survived without her. She listened to me as I talked through what happened over and over again trying to make sense of what was happening in my marriage. She was there for me, when I cried so hard and spiraled into panic attacks. She brought food and encouraged me to eat and stay strong. She was just there. I had lost my person, and she promised to be my person until I found a new one — and she was the best person God could have substituted in for me. Little did she know when she promised that I would still be single five years later, would move into her basement during Covid, and live with her for six months. (*Sorry, not sorry. Love you.*)

For the first handful of months I called her multiple times a day and every night before bed when the loneliness hit the hardest. The nights were always the worst when I would work myself up so much I needed her to help calm me down with promises that I would be okay —that I would make it through to the other side and one day, be happy again.

I began to notice that with all of my friends I became this draining ball of negative energy. I felt it, and bless their souls, they stuck through it with me in those awful times when my misery was all we could talk about.

I remember one of my therapists introducing me to the concept of energy for the first time, explaining how we sense the joy and lightness of a happy person and the heaviness and sadness of an unhappy person. Also, how this energy can attract like-energy people and push away others.

I started becoming really cognizant of this after my best friend's husband told her she needed to stop getting so involved in my separation and how that energy and heaviness was affecting her and their family. That hit hard, I couldn't lose her or them.

1. My Hired Best Friend

January 2019, I was on a weekend retreat with a ladies forum. It was actually a spousal forum within the Entrepreneurs Organization my husband was a member of. I had been with this same group of ladies for two years and they had been major confidants and sources of stability for me in Arizona the year of my separation. It was my first official event that I co-planned with one of my forum-mates.

I did some research to bring in a private yoga instructor to the mansion we rented in La Jolla, California for the weekend and found a beautiful soul that was the perfect fit, Ava. I fell in love with her energy and calmness. A couple weeks later I hired her as a life/transformation coach. Therapists were tough for me. I felt like I was constantly spinning wheels, in a negative feedback loop, and wanted help to see the future versus focusing on the past.

Hiring Ava was one of the best investments I've ever made in myself. She focused on self-love practices like breathwork, meditation, tapping, and spirituality practices to help me create new routines and perspectives. She basically became my paid best friend. I would call or text her when I was having overwhelming emotions and needed support.

Knowing when it was time to hire someone to get support beyond what I was getting from my friends and family was key to sustaining those very relationships, and finally becoming the person they looked forward to spending time with again instead of that grey cloud of despair.

None of my friends were divorced, so it was difficult for them to know what I was feeling and experiencing. They could show me compassion, but weren't able to empathize. The first couple months after a separation everyone is in it with you. They're available for calls, ready to be with you at a moment's notice. Then your situation becomes old news to them even when you're still deep in the process of grieving. So either finding a community of divorced people who understand what it feels like, or hiring a bestie where you have regular calls works really well.

Paying for a mentor or coach keeps the boundaries open between you and your friends so it doesn't affect those relationships and you still have someone in your corner to talk about the tough stuff with so you can begin to release and heal.

Throughout the rest of this book are tidbits of magic Ava introduced me to that completely changed me as a person. I owe her so much for rocketing me onto the path I'm on today. She gave me the foundation to find my strength and keep climbing.

2. Therapists/Counselors

Finding a good therapist or counselor that you connect with and can provide you with value for your particular situation is hard. Finding a therapist that is familiar with separation and divorce is even tougher. Non-specialized therapists may have their own biases on marriage that trickle into your sessions that can often be more damaging. (*Learned the hard way.*) This is why I had more success in growing and transforming into my new single-self with a coach versus a traditional therapist.

I grew up and lived most of my life in a small town where we don't talk about our problems, let alone pay someone else to do that with. There was the mentality that there is something deeply wrong with you if you were seeing a therapist and mental health was seen as complete taboo.

Right after he left, I started driving three hours to the "city" to have access to mental health services. My therapist was incredible, and I needed her those first couple months. She reminded me what my morals and values were and really took me back to the basics of self-love. She also came from a Christian point of view, which really resonated with my soul. But, she was three hours away and driving in for a two to three hour session every week or two was difficult to sustain long term. Then I moved to Arizona and phone therapy sessions just weren't the same.

The annoying and frustrating part about finding the perfect therapist is that you have to tell your story. OVER AND OVER AND OVER AGAIN. Which was honestly too much for me. Going to the therapist was so mentally exhausting, especially after a couple of bad experiences, I didn't want to go back.

But, the right therapist or counselor can be life-saving if it is a better fit for you and your situation. Remember, this journey is yours and whatever feels good and right for you.

3. Retreats

The reality pause, that break from reality that retreats provide is severely undermined and undervalued. We live in a time where there's always something next, something to plan, something to think about. Sitting down to meditate for 10 undistracted minutes can even be challenging, let alone finding the time to do some deep inner work. Not to say that taking a break from reality can't be done at home, for some. I am one of those people with an untamable monkey brain that has never been able to master the art of doing nothing, so for me retreats have been life-changing. And I mean that literally. These retreats changed my life.

I dive into my retreat experiences more in chapter 9. There are so many nuggets of wisdom I learned at each retreat. I want to share my learnings and experiences with you to help you find the lessons in them. So more on that to come.

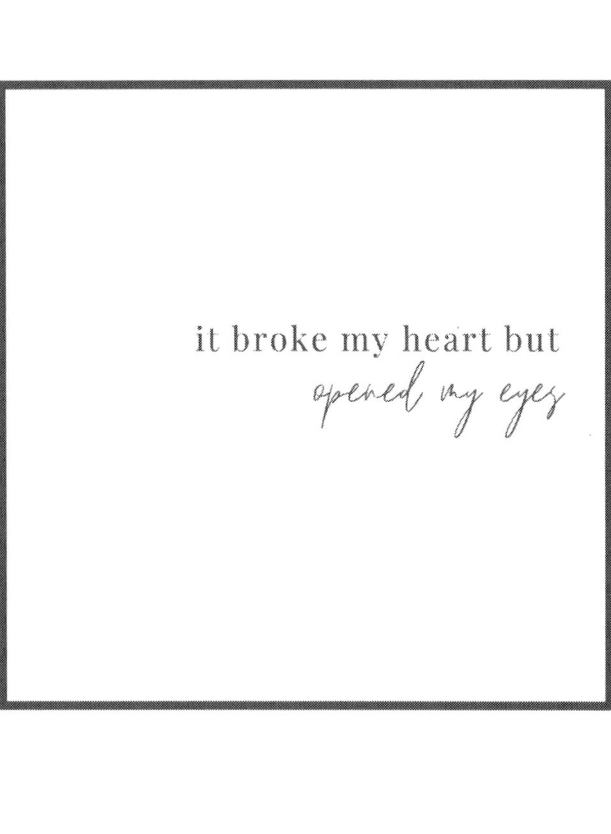
it broke my heart but
opened my eyes

Chapter 7

Who Am I?

Mantra: *I love and appreciate myself*

Who am I?

For years I couldn't answer this question. I was my marriage, and I lived for our life. I loved hard, maybe too hard, and I buried myself so deep in my relationship I forgot who Steph was. I was a we, not a me.

When he left, my identity was taken and I felt as though I was relabeled as "divorced" which screamed FAILURE to me. So, I had to rediscover myself.

But, let's just stop and think about this for a second. How powerful is it that we GET this time to ourselves to work on ourselves, for ourselves. Yes, the circumstances absolutely suck and it's not what we want at all. Accepting this new reality, that this is life now, allows us a perspective shift that can be a huge opportunity for personal growth and development. We get a chance to date ourselves, spoil ourselves, do only the things WE like to do, figure out what we dislike and choose not to do them if we don't want to, and everything in between. It's a period of re-learning that can be so beautiful if we let it. We get to remember ourselves, find her again, and LOVE HER. Discover what SHE likes and doesn't like, without anyone else's input or influence. Try out new restaurants, learn a new skill or hobby, take yourself to a movie, a concert, go out hiking and explore a new trail. Take the time, because it can truly be a gift. And it will be incredibly important in preparing yourself for your next relationship OR just the next chapter of life and, to enter it truly in-tune with yourself.

Here are some of the things I learned though dating myself and diving deep into who I am:

My Morals and Values

Our morals and values are the guiding points of our life. Our true north.

During one of my first therapy sessions I was led through an exercise to hone in on my morals and values. The therapist called this exercise "cups." She had a little bag of paper slips that listed a moral or value on it and two plastic cups labeled A and B. Together we went through each paper slip and I would add it to either Cup A or Cup B. Cup A was for a moral or value that was important to me, Cup B was the discard pile of what didn't resonate. After you've gone through the bag, you then empty out Cup A and go through it again until you're left with what works out to be your top 10 morals and values. Then prioritize these one through 10. How do you feel when looking at this list? I know for me those ten slips of paper just felt... right. Like me.

The second part of this exercise is to then look at your top five morals and values and ask yourself:

1: Are you living in alignment with your morals and values? If not, what are some shifts you can make to live a life within your top five. When we are living in alignment with what matters most to us we feel more fulfilled and grounded in ourselves.

2: Does your ex spouse/partner live within your top morals and values?

This can be an interesting question to answer. And some follow-up questions to percolate on: Do you want to be with someone who doesn't share the same morals and values as you? Would you ever be truly happy with someone who doesn't share the same morals and values as you?

The purpose of this exercise is to illustrate that you will never be truly happy, as an individual or in a relationship, if you are not aligned with what matters most to you or how you intuitively live your life based on your morals and values. You have to be comfortable with the actions and choices you make and it will have a significant impact on your happiness.

Making Decisions

I hadn't made a decision for myself or by myself in the last six years. I couldn't trust myself to make the right choice and I would spin myself into a tangled web of anxiety trying to do so.

This was hard, and I learned too there was a lot about adulting that I didn't know and had to learn for the first time at the age of 29. Accounting, taxes, and budgeting, to name a few. I was so fortunate to not have to think or even worry about those things for my whole adult life. It was scary and overwhelming and I felt incredibly stupid. I didn't know what I didn't know, and because there were so many things I didn't know, I had a very difficult time trusting myself to know what the right decision was.

What was even harder was to swallow my pride, take a deep breath, and ask for help if I needed. There is zero shame in that. There is zero shame in taking your time, leaning into your intuition to what your gut feeling tells you. Trusting yourself again takes baby-steps.

My Place in the World

It took me a long time to find my place in the world again. I even dedicated 16 months of my life to figuring it out as I lived in my best-friend's basement and Airbnb-hopped my way around various British Columbia cities to find a fit. Working remotely gave me this freedom, for which I was very fortunate, but my very wise best friend once said to me, "You never have to stay in a place you don't want to." I took that advice to heart. I wanted to find my ***home*** again.

Even after those 16 months of bouncing around, it still doesn't feel as though I've found my "home" in physical form yet. It's almost as if I've left my heart in different places around the world that have meant so much to me on this journey: Scottsdale, Sedona, Victoria, Whistler, Kelowna, Summerland. Each of them gives me a piece of my dream or ideal lifestyle, but I haven't found the full picture yet. I have learned that, just like Najwa Zebian is quoted in "Alone," *I have created a home within myself*. Wherever my dogs are, our little unit is our home, and we've created an adaptable lifestyle that allows us to make a home wherever we are. And for now, I know it's all I need and that level of freedom has given me choices that my wanderlust heart felt deprived of for so long.

My Inner Child

A practice that I love to spend time in is inner child work. It involves getting in touch with a younger version of yourself in meditation. I had no idea how powerful it was to go back to visit three year old little Steph who was extremely shy but oh so goofy and loving. Spending time with her has left me feeling incredibly protective over her and empowered to move forward in a way that honors that little girl inside. Lately, inner child work has taken me back to 29 year old Steph on the day her husband told her he was leaving. Experiencing that again but in third person is deep work, and again left me so protective over this fragile shell version of myself that I am now determined to keep safe from harm again.

These inner child practices—done with therapists, counselors, or alone via guided meditations—to get in touch with a previous version of myself by looking back through a bystanders perspective, have been very healing for me and made me stronger in my self worth.

Give Yourself a Free Day

At least once a week, when I'm able to, I give myself a free day. It is typically a Sunday where I have no plans, no schedule to meet, just a day to be. I've found this so healthy for my emotional and mental well-being. I'll wake up, have a slow morning and ask myself what I need that day. What does my body, mind, and soul need before a new week or to recoup from the previous one. Some days this looks like just laying on the couch and ordering take out. Other free days it's a roadtrip to a new part of the city or local area I haven't visited when I just need to go for a drive. Following my intuition this way has led to finding some of the best coffee shops, random waterfalls, or just an epic view from the top of a hike I've been wanting to do because I needed a day in the forest with the dogs. It's also been a great way to allow myself to explore, be playful, and learn a little more about myself through these adventures.

This is such a big act of self-love that you can give to yourself so freely, to build your intuition, and to continue to learn about yourself.

My Expanders

Jealousy can be a dirty little bugger when you're already down in the dumps and looking at friends or people on social media who seemingly have it all. For a while, every time I saw a happy couple strolling the streets holding hands I would roll my eyes. Until I was introduced to the expanders exercise. This goes hand-in-hand with the neuro-linguistic programming (NLP) I'll be touching on later, but the basis of finding your expanders is turning envy into wishful possibilities for the future.

An expander is a person, couple, influencer, or someone similar that is inspirational for you. They have or do something that you aspire to.

The practice includes writing an ongoing list of these six categories:

- Love/Relationship
- Career
- Family
- Spirituality/Personal Development
- Lifestyle

And under each category write down the expanders, those people that you look up to that exemplify that category or goals that you aspire to.

For the love and relationship category, I know of four couples who have marriages and relationships with their spouse that I deeply admire and can't wait to have one day with my future spouse. They are all on my expanders list. As an event producer, I was putting on a workshop for my celebrity coaching clients and one of them walked in, put down her Louis Vuitton briefcase and took off her Louboutin high-heels before going up on stage. She has been on my career expanders list for four years now (one day!). Think of your list as a who-do-I-want-to-be-when-I-grow-up list for different aspects of your life. So not only is it a powerful manifesting practice it is also a jealousy buster by switching the language from envy to expansion.

Be a Mirror for Love

Love is the reason why this season hurts so much. There is a lot of love for a person that you can no longer give it to and it feels so empty. A really powerful self-love meditation I was guided through on my healing journey focused on mirroring the love I have for others back to myself.

My personal preference is always guided meditation, even after years of practice I still suck at meditating to get into a theta state. But here is the outline of the meditation if you are able to guide yourself through this journey.

Sitting or laying down comfortably, close your eyes and clear your mind. Allow yourself to be present. Take four to five deep belly breaths. Then begin to think of the person you love you love most in the world. Picture them standing in front of you and all the love that you have for this being is in the form of a light. What color is it? Picture that light pouring out of you and towards that person engulfing them in your love. Feel that love, sit in it for a moment. Now replace the image of the person you're imagining with a mirror, and watch as that mirror reflects your love back to you. Feel all that love coating you, wrapping you up like a cozy blanket. Sit in that love for as long as you want.

YOU created that love, and just as easily as you can give it to others, you can give it to yourself.

Be Your Most Authentic Self

One major gift I've learned through this chapter of life is how my best, most authentic self is so loved that I cry for the version of myself that was kept in a box and stifled for so long. Learning about yourself and honoring it comes with the freedom to explore, to be unapologetic, to be accountable to no one but yourself, and how you move into this next chapter of your life.

For me, I am a stand for kindness and generosity. I am a stand for love, for truth, and for honesty. I stand for each individual's uniqueness and the gifts we bring to the world. I stand for vulnerability and sharing our experiences to help others.

Take a moment, take a deep breath and ask yourself ***what do you stand for***.

I love this question because a "stand" is your mission, it's what you believe in. Let's twist that big question into one focused on future relationships. After all that you've been through, do you still believe in love? In marriage? In loyalty and commitment? In taking the higher road?

Whatever it is, stay true to that. Because just as our morals and values are our true north, what we stand for will guide us to our sense of self and how we navigate new paths in the next chapter. *What do you stand for?* Stay true to that.

i will never have this version of me again

let me slow down and be with her

rupi kaur

Chapter 8

Reality Pause

Mantra: *I am here*

Other than massages every once in a while, I had done very limited self-care and personal development. It wasn't common where I grew up in small-town Saskatchewan. Rarely did people invest in themselves or spend money on things to take care of their emotional or mental well-being. And if they did, it was most certainly not shared or talked about. At least it wasn't in my family or friend group. My ex invested a lot into his own personal and professional development, and throughout our marriage encouraged me to do the same. I don't know why I was so resistant when we were together but I believe it was a mix of fear of the unknown, guilt of spending money on myself (not seeing my own personal development worthiness), and insecurity holding me back.

One of my girlfriends, whom I had confided in early in my separation, shared about a private and personalized retreat in Sedona, Arizona she had just been on that was life changing for her. I knew I needed something to help me make sense of what was going on, to help me think straight, help me know that everything was going to be okay—that I was going to be okay.

I had some money saved up so I booked myself a week at the same retreat center she had told me about, SpiritQuest.

This was the beginning of my love affair for retreats. The opportunity to have a little pause from reality to do a deep dive into myself, my dreams, and, in my case, just dealing with my present reality without other life distractions. The value that I gained from each retreat was priceless and they taught me a lot of the tools that I'm sharing in this book.

Life is too busy. We're constantly surrounded by so much noise and stressors, never mind tackling a traumatic separation and divorce amidst all of that. It's a lot to process. And on a guided retreat where you can be vulnerable with yourself and others is such an expansive experience.

SpiritQuest, Sedona AZ

SpiritQuest in Sedona, Arizona is a unique facility that creates private and personalized retreats with a faculty of highly-trained professionals and self-care practitioners to guide you on a healing journey. I called into SpiritQuest, told them what was going on in my life, what I needed and was hoping from a retreat, and they formulated a personalized plan of different therapy sessions and alternative healing modalities that build off of and support one another. I booked seven intense days, with three sessions a day.

I went completely offline that week. No phone or internet at all, for any reason. I sat with myself, journalled, and cried and cried and cried. I slept, ate well, and spent as much time outside in the desert as possible. I can truly say that this retreat was a pivotal moment in my healing journey. It was early enough in my separation that everything was super raw and the practitioners provided me with tools that got me through the extremely rough following year. It was not a fix-all, I still went through a deep, deep depression after that, but I do think these self-soothing practices are what saved me from falling into the deep end most days.

I went into this emotional healing retreat having just signed a separation agreement and understanding that my life would be in limbo for the next 10 months of separation. Hoping and praying for that one percent chance that he would change his mind and come home to me and the dogs.

Each state in America is a little different on their divorce laws. In Arizona, you could file and be divorced the next month. But being Canadian citizens, we had to be separated for a full year before he could file for divorce. So doing this retreat in Arizona had created some biases on marriage with the therapists I worked with that were vastly different points of view than my own. Looking back now, this was the beginning of finding my voice and using it.

The value I received during these seven days is indescribable. I could write a whole chapter on this retreat alone, but I've condensed it into easily usable pieces for you to consider for your own healing and replicate for yourself if they fit for you.

Release

My SpiritQuest retreat started off with a release ceremony, and as simple as it was, it was equally powerful. The facilitator drove us out to Boynton Canyon, outside of West Sedona and we climbed up a small trail so we could get a good view of the valley below, the area where the red rocks met the desert plain. We each took a seat on large boulders, and looked out at the vastness below. I shared with her what was going on, we did a guided meditation, and then just sat in silence for a long time. I set an intention for the retreat, and sat in my current reality. Then I chose a rock, and pulsed all of my grief, anger, and confusion into that rock and threw it as far as I could. One rock didn't seem like enough, so I did it again. That second rock symbolized the perfection I was letting go, and returning to being a fully authentic human loving my flaws and accepting the mistakes I've made.

This was the first time I let go of some of the blame that I was carrying feeling that it was all my fault that he left.

As we were getting up to leave that spot, I looked down and saw a large heart shaped rock protruding out of the ground, and I realized that was my sign. Love was always my end-goal and seeing hearts, representing love, was a sign that I would be okay. My simple reminder. Then I found a rock nearby that caught my eye. I wouldn't throw this one and instead put it in my pocket to keep as a reminder of that ceremony. It still sits on my bookshelf today.

Accept

A key part of this retreat, and the goal of my practitioners, was to get me to accept what was going on in my marriage. But to me, accepting felt like giving up. It felt like a minimizing word that was a complete disservice to myself, my morals, my values, and my marriage vows. That I was okay with what was happening. I had a very very hard time accepting my new reality.

The actual definition of acceptance surprised me because I had been using it the wrong way for years. *Acceptance is the ability to acknowledge the reality of a situation without resistance.*

I was definitely resisting my new reality in the early months, which explains why acceptance felt like such a dirty word. It wasn't until one of my practitioners at SpiritQuest helped me see that our relationship was over as I knew it because it had changed. It would never go back to how it was before he left. **That is what I needed to accept**. In the instance that we did come back together it would be a new relationship because of what we both went through in the separation. Also, I likely wouldn't accept the old version of our relationship because I changed and now knew that I wanted and deserved more in a marriage. That is something I was able to accept.

Meditate

At least one session a day was a therapy session that would start off with a three to five minute meditation. This was the first time I actually meditated and it felt so good to just give my brain a dedicated amount of time to not think. I would say to myself that I wasn't allowed to worry or think for the next x amount of time and that I was safe to just be. It would calm my monkey mind knowing that I was safe in that moment to shed myself of my worries and fears, even for just a couple minutes. Through this, I was able to put my guard down.

Breathe

The first time I was introduced to breathwork was at SpiritQuest and I knew right away it was a powerful form of medicine for me. This variety of breathwork is unique. The practitioner used a mixture of loud music, sacred aboriginal songs and spiritual chants, and his own instruments that I could feel the vibrations of, like a didgeridoo, chimes, and sound bowls. He would also use feathers to create a wind like motion that swept across my body. This combination of produced music, his instruments, the physical sensation of the feathers, and the breathwork exercise he led me through in rhythm to the music created a fully immersive experience.

Breathwork is so beneficial to our bodies, including aiding in relieving stress and anxiety, reducing physiological stress, and healing trauma. I experience major internal and emotional release when I do breathwork, often bawling my eyes out, which I need as someone who doesn't express emotions very easily and holds a lot in.

Language

A couple of my sessions were with a Neuro-Linguistic Programming (NLP) practitioner which was surprisingly one of the most impactful sessions I had at SpiritQuest. I needed to change my internal dialogue of blaming myself for him leaving and the doomsday approach I was taking in my separation. Basically, I needed to be kinder to myself.

A super simple but impactful practice she taught me was correcting my self-sabotage. I like to call it the "Oopsie Daisy." Anytime you catch yourself in negative inner dialogue, over-worrying, or thinking something sad or awful, put on your tiniest, squeakiest, goofiest child voice and say "OOPSIE DAISY! I fell," and picture the negative thinking as the act of falling down. First of all, saying oopsie daisy is silly and ridiculous and chances are you can't say it with a straight face. Then follow that thought by saying "It's okay. I'm okay. Everyone does it."

We all fall. But correcting ourselves by getting back up, brushing it off, and forgiving ourselves is key to changing the negativity.

Another NLP hack this practitioner taught me, that I re-learned multiple times through watching the movie, *The Secret,* and reading Gabby Bernstein's work, is always speaking in manifesting language —which is really the language of desire and possibility. Always putting out into the universe (or God, based on your spirituality) what you want. For example, removing "if" and replacing it with "when."

"If I ever get married again" changes into "When I get married again." If you want to eventually be in another relationship that leads to marriage, let the universe know that.

Or, referring back to the "Who Am I?" chapter on jealousy. The shift of "Why do they have what I want," into "I can't wait to have that, too," is so powerful in shifting towards a possibility mindset.

Also, by making your "nos" strong NOs and "yeses" strong YESes let's the universe know what you actually want. So often we use contradictory language that could be really confusing in relaying what we really want. Especially during this time of separation and divorce when all I wanted was my husband to come back, I had to really self-evaluate what I was saying and feeling through OOPSIE DAISY moments.

For example, I could turn "I don't want to be sad anymore," into "I want to be happy and light." I am essentially saying the same thing, but only saying it positively. This tricks your brain into focusing on the positive word and statement versus the negative word that can keep you in the darkness.

Self-Soothing

The NLP practitioner was so full of wisdom. I absolutely adored my sessions with her. In addition to learning how to speak kindly to myself, she guided me on a super simple and potent self-soothing practice that I use regularly.

Our bodies react at an instinctive and unconscious level to touch and pressure that can help soothe our parasympathetic nervous system which allows us to rest. Similar to what I've already mentioned by taking a warm bath, getting a massage, or emotional freedom technique/tapping.

Either sitting back or laying down, take one of your hands (whichever feels most natural) and lay it across your chest. Align your middle finger with your nipple and slightly spread out your fingers. Then take your other hand and place it just underneath the other along the lower half of your chest, touching your thumb to the pinky finger of the first hand. That's it! It's that simple. Stay in the position for as long as it feels comfortable and experience a calming warmth wash over your body. A diagram of this is shown on parableofabrokenheart.com/resources to help you visualize.

The pressure from your hands in this position across your chest acts somewhat like a hug, triggering our body to feel safe and slows down our nervous system into a mode of rest. Whenever I'm having a stressful day and need to take a break, or if I'm having trouble sleeping I will use this self-soothing technique and it works like a charm every time.

Scent Memory

Upon arriving at SpiritQuest they handed me a welcome package that included a little purple velvet pouch with a small vial of essential oils. The receptionist then introduced me to scent memory and that SpiritQuest created their own essential oil blend that would act as a reminder of my experience there. Scent is a powerful source of memory, like how fresh baked bread reminds me of my grandmother everytime I smell it, or that specific scent of my grandfather's hair oil that takes me right back to my grandparents farm. The SpiritQuest blend was a mix of juniper, sage, and something sweet that I can't remember, but at the beginning of every session at SpiritQuest I would take a deep inhale of the blend. Now, for the last five years, whenever I'm feeling overwhelmed, anxious, or depressed about life (because it still does happen) I'll come across my special essential oil blend from SpiritQuest and just smelling it brings me back to the calming energy of my time there and the power I discovered in myself to get through hard things.

I encourage you to find a scent that really resonates with this period of time. It might be a specific candle scent or a room spray you love. Light it, spray it, or smell it whenever you sit down to do healing work. Use it as a ritual and the scent memory will develop to be associated with this transitional season and hopefully remind you just how powerful and resilient you are.

Rest in Nature

I'm a big outdoors person. I love hiking, being out on the water paddle boarding or kayaking, snowboarding or skiing in the winter. At SpiritQuest I worked with a Shaman, another first for me. What I love most about Shamanism is that deep connection with nature and our interconnectedness with the earth. With the Shaman I did deep meditations, learned about plant medicine and animal guides, sat in ceremony among the red rocks honoring the land and asking for its support. One of the reasons Sedona is such a sacred place for me now is because of my work with that Shaman. He guided me to learn to lean on mother earth for love and protection and using nature as a form of mental and emotional medicine that I really resonated with. At the core, it amplified my appreciation for nature and reminded me of how I feel when I'm out in the forest, alongside a rugged beach, meeting up with an animal on a trail, and the sense of oneness that comes with just being.

If you aren't familiar with Cathedral Rock in Sedona, I invite you to pause and look it up right now so you have a visual of what I'm about to share. I unfortunately only had one session with this sweet soul of a woman who took me on a red rock hike overlooking Cathedral Rock. After a 15 minute hike into the desert we came upon a huge piece of slick rock where we laid our mats down on the red rock. I was completely enamored with Cathedral Rock. I couldn't keep my eyes off of it as we moved through a gentle yoga flow, It was magnetizing.

At the end of the session, the yogi introduced me to the symbolism of Cathedral Rock. In the middle there are two spires that rise up and resemble a man and a woman with their backs together. The Hopi people, a local Native American tribe, say that this man and this woman symbolize a true partnership where a couple will always have each other's backs.

Many times in my first year of separation while living in Scottsdale I would drive out to Sedona, back to that big slab of slick rock and just sit looking up at Cathedral Rock. Praying and meditating that one day I will have a new relationship that truly embraces the teachings of this sacred space.

Living in Love Versus Fear

A big lesson and mindset shift I learned at SpiritQuest is that we navigate life, make choices, decisions, and think our thoughts from one of the two primary emotions, love or fear. These two core emotions underlie every other emotion we have. We are either coming from a place of love or fear, light or darkness, and neither can exist in the presence of the other. This was a teaching introduced to me at SpiritQuest but reiterated in A Course in Miracles, another special practice in my healing journey.

Think about this for a second: in your current situation are you in a place of love or fear? I know when I was in my separation I was in a constant state of fear. Fear of what to do, terrified of what's coming next, how I was going to survive on a single income... So. Much. Fear. I was in a constant state of it.

Fear paralyzes us, it holds us back with all encompassing stress and anxiety. Whereas love brings us peace and sets us free.

Other Retreats:

Since SpiritQuest I've gone on retreats in Nosara, Costa Rica, Sacred Valley, Peru, Big Sur, California and another back in Sedona. Now I know I need to take a retreat at least once a year to take that pause from reality and get back to myself. A retreat for me turns into a constant state of meditation where I allow myself to just be, dream, and receive guidance on next steps. It is a powerful gift we can give ourselves to take a reality pause.

you don't know this new me;
I put my pieces back *differently*

Chapter 9

Create a Safe Space

Mantra: *I am ready to be healed*

Journal Entry - January 16, 2020

I was unpacking some boxes earlier this week and stumbled across some half-used journals in my box of books. I thought I had "cleaned" these out during my last move (AKA ripped out all of the used pages) which in my mind would deem the journals "usable" again.

In doing so I accidentally flipped to one of the pages in an old journal that listed out my 2018 New Year's resolutions and goals.

It was a full page where I had sectioned out work, family, relationship, personal, and spiritual resolutions. At the top of the page it showed that my word of year was Courage. To have the courage to be me, to say what I mean, to share how I feel, to say no, and do what makes me happy.

This was from before he left, only seven months before he left and right after we had an amazing Christmas at home and a fun New Years' Eve together celebrating love and life. The life I only live now in my dreams.

I had a pretty shitty day mood wise and when I stopped long enough to have my own thoughts on this busy work day they would immediately float back to this list. Especially the "family" section that said:

"Start our own family"

2018 was supposed to be our year to build.

We had talked about kids for years. We always wanted a family, but the timing never seemed right. For the first five years of marriage we led such busy lifestyles with lots of travel, focusing on work and snowbirding between Arizona and Saskatchewan. I wanted more stability before we started our family.

Then over Christmas 2017 it hit me. Baby fever hit me hard and 2018 was going to be our year. My husband wasn't traveling as much anymore for work, I was working from home, and we had settled into our own place in Arizona. Everything finally felt right.

I would find myself daydreaming about it all. Him playing with our kids like he did with our dogs. It was so adorable and melted my heart just thinking about it. I wanted to make him a daddy so badly. There was nothing more I wanted than our own family.

This one-pager from my journal knocked me back a couple of steps for sure. Maybe a whole staircase. My biggest concern at that time was being more mindful of my spending and planning out my pregnancy. A lifetime ago that I barely recognize but also feels so right and at home at the same time.

Right now, I'd give anything to go back to writing out that list at the beginning of 2018. Little did I know that I was battling major depression at that time, but a family had given me something to look forward to.

I had been doing manifesting meditations, positive mindset work, journalling —all the things to help me move forward, and I've been feeling good. But after seeing that unpleasant reminder I've fallen deeply into sadness, anger and fear. It was a reminder that I'm starting all over again. From scratch. I had it all. Everything that I had ever wanted and so much excitement about entering the next chapter of our lives as parents. But he didn't want that and certainly not with me. What we had talked and dreamed about for so long turned out to only be one-sided. That rejection is like a knife twisting in my heart.

I couldn't imagine having gone through what I did during this separation and divorce with kids.

But, nonetheless. It still hurts. It hurts a lot.

When I moved from Arizona to Victoria after our separation for a fresh start, I was very cognizant not to bring anything that reminded me of him. I sold the few furniture pieces I kept from our lake house, and any items that I wasn't able to yet get rid of I kept in the garage until I could sell them. That house, my fresh start, was my sanctuary. My safe place and I wasn't allowing any negative energy from the divorce into that space.

I feel so lucky that I was able to give myself this fresh start and had my parents support to help move me back to Canada. I know not many are as fortunate to move cities, or countries to escape memories, but there are little things you can do to make your space feel refreshed and safe from triggers. This could be in the form of rearranging furniture or getting rid of any pieces that particularly hold triggering memories. This could go for clothing as well. These are all materialistic things and are replaceable. Your emotional health is more important than those things that bring you sadness.

I read somewhere the power of releasing emotional ties to objects when you watch them burn. I don't know if I enjoyed the permission from this to dip into my love of burning shit, and I definitely did not look at my gated community's handbook before buying a metal garbage bin and burning all of the books, pictures, pieces of clothing I had that reminded me of him in the driveway. My best friend who lived next door came over and we sat in lawn chairs poking and stirring the fire with metal BBQ tongs, and chugging champagne right from the bottle. Classy, but boy did that ever feel good.

I did the same the next time I went to my parents. I had a large plastic tote of wedding pictures, our invitations, my bridal shoes, cards, love letters, and memorabilia from our relationship. My parents had an actual burning barrel in their yard, so I emptied the tote, soaked everything in gasoline, threw in a match and watched it burn. My dad definitely thought I was a little psychotic, but it was very therapeutic.

Visual triggers can also be in your social media. The first six months of my separation I went on a social media detox. I was fairly active on my Instagram and Facebook accounts beforehand but I had zero energy to be involved in that picture perfect world while I was going through a personal crisis. That break was so needed. When I eventually got back on, I was overwhelmed by all of the triggers. Pictures, videos, and my own posting history. My best friend offered to go through my Facebook and Instagram for me to remove any pictures, but after much consideration of her generous offer I decided it was something I needed to do myself. I dedicated a full afternoon to scrounging through all of my platforms, removing the images of us, of him. It was somewhat ceremonial. I also did this to my camera roll in my phone.

Eventually I had to unfollow and remove followers from my social media that were also triggers. This may have included people and friends that I still loved, or had zero negative experiences with, but they were triggers nonetheless through the images they shared or by tagging my ex, and for my mental and emotional stability, if I wanted to continue on social media, I had to cut those ties too.

You can't erase someone from your life completely, and I honestly didn't want to. We had made some incredible memories together throughout our relationship. It just hurt too much to continuously see these reminders, which was my reason for the purge. But when I come across a picture now that I missed in the cleanse I pause and honor that memory, I feel into that moment, and let myself remember it in a happy way. Then I delete it.

Verbal triggers are even more unpredictable than the visual ones. Especially when coming from others.

For probably the first nine months after we separated, my friends, family, and I talked in depth about my separation, and I needed to because I was still processing and needed their support to help me work through all the changes. But it came to a point where I realized how unhealthy it was for me to keep spinning the story in circles and keeping tabs on what he was up to. I had to set some major boundaries with my friends and family. I couldn't know anything that was going on with my ex. He removed me from his social media about six months after he left, and I refused to look him up to see what he was up to. I knew it wouldn't be healthy for me. It happened a couple times when he was casually brought up in conversation, about something he had posted on instagram and I would go down a rabbit hole of despair. For my own mental health and well-being, I needed to create a safe space for myself around hearing about his life—even in casual conversation.

We have to create these boundaries with our people. Let them know we don't want to know that kind of information and please not share it any more. Let them know you're still hurting and sharing what he is doing is the opposite of helping. This isn't gossip, it's your life.

Friends, especially, can be a bad influence on your healing. I recall a couple situations where some girlfriends encouraged me to go out drinking and partying to get my mind off things. That was no longer a part of my life and I knew that even if I had fun in the moment, that it wasn't aligned with who I was and it wouldn't be beneficial for me long term. It may actually make things worse. So when your friends offer up suggestions to help you, make sure that you're staying true to yourself and the way you're comfortable healing and processing. It's okay to turn down their suggestions and instead let them know how you need to be supported.

you've always had the power
my dear, you just had to
learn it for yourself

Glinda, the Good Witch of the North
The Wizard of Oz

Chapter 10

What Else You Lose

Mantra: *I am resilient*

Journal Entry: May 9, 2020

It's something I had been dreading for the last year and a half. Going home.

You see, my hometown was also "our" town. Where our story started. Where we blossomed and bloomed. Where we dreamed together and made our best memories.

My friends and family all picked and poked at me, not understanding why I was having such a hard time facing that town. How could they understand? I couldn't really expect anyone who hasn't gone through the kind of trauma that I have to fully understand.

Yes, I grew up in that small, small rural Saskatchewan town. Those were just as much my people and places as his. But it wasn't like that.

It was ***the memories of us that haunted me*** *that I wasn't sure if I was able to face.*

The pandemic had a way of really bringing out the single in me. After week four of self-isolation I was so completely lonely. I craved human interaction like never before. My best friend realized how unhealthy it was getting for me and invited me to come stay with her and her family to ease the loneliness and spend time with them.

Just days after she first mentioned it I had my car packed up, dogs in tow, and we made the 2000+ kilometer journey back to Saskatchewan from Vancouver Island. My parents agreed to watch the dogs for me while I stayed with my friends, but only under the condition that I drop them off and stay a couple days with them at my childhood farm just outside the town I grew up in and the town I had lived with my ex in until he left.

The thought of it made me sick. It was no disrespect to my parents, the life they provided me or the beautiful farm I grew up on. It was dreading all of the memories I hadn't faced yet that I still wasn't sure I was ready for.

I was in such a good place. I was truly happy. Sure, I still have some bad days, but they were far and few between. I didn't want to hurt again.

I tried to plan out a route where I didn't have to go through town to get to the farm. But any which way included either a 45 minute detour or driving down mucky grid roads that I didn't want to take my car down.

It was dark by the time I rolled in. I had been mentally preparing myself for hours.

The closest I had got was last summer, when I stopped at the next town over to visit my grandmother. That was also the time I was served divorce papers in her care home facility. Those memories burned in me as I drove through that sleepy town.

As I came over the hill and saw the lights of my hometown for the first time, my heart and breath stopped. Within milliseconds I was flooded with all sorts of emotions and I had to pull over on the side of the road because I was crying so hard. I sat parked on the side of the road and sobbed harder than I had in months for about 15 minutes. I couldn't stop.

When I finally got control over myself, I messaged my best friend. "It hurts too much" and she gave me encouraging words, like she had since he left. I started up my vehicle again and carried on.

I crawled through town. Memories hitting me from all angles, stabbing me in the heart with a dull butter knife over and over and over.

Passing by our old storage compound on the other side of town, then the airplane hanger with the old family company logo where I knew our boat, my snowmobile, and our other toys that we created the best memories were stored had me stop again.

This was worse than I had expected to react.

I knew the worst was yet to come, so I gathered up the strength to continue down the highway.

Thank God the roads were quiet.

I hadn't had a panic attack like that since the first weeks after he left. It hit me so hard and so fast I couldn't breathe. The first time I saw our acreage. Our first home together. A beautiful brick home on the side of the highway, with a driveway curving over a creek into a perfectly manicured yard lined with a white fence. It hadn't changed one bit.

I pulled over again just past the driveway so the new owners couldn't see me stopped. I was crying so hard I had to get out to vomit.

This was unbearable.

This is where we lived our happiest years. Our wedding pictures were taken in that yard. We battled with our driveway every spring with flooded water from the creek, and in the winter plowed through the biggest snow drifts. I spent hours cutting grass in the summer months.

Where I epically failed in planting my first garden with my mother-in-law. It was the home we brought our dogs Beau and Finn home to. Where we hosted my parents 25th wedding anniversary party, and many other get-togethers.

In the three years I had lived there with him, it was home.

I couldn't move for what seemed like hours. I just sat there and sobbed uncontrollably.

When I was finally able to move, we continued down the road another five minutes to my parents farm. See - it was THAT close. Far too close for comfort.

I turned where I would have otherwise continued to the lake where we had built a new home not even five years ago. I'm not sure if I would ever be ready to face that place.

Of course, my parents didn't understand when I got there with a mascara streaked face and blood-shot eyes. "Well, you'll just have to get over it." Thanks.

I headed down the hallway to my childhood bedroom and instantly saw that my wedding gown was still hanging in the closet. As soon as I saw the pink bag I took a deep breath and kindly asked my dad to remove it promptly from the room and put it in the basement. That really sucked too.

I was happy to be there, I loved my parents farm. My dogs loved it more and would be taken such good care of by my parents while I took the time I needed to go be with friends.

I didn't leave the farm for a couple days until I left to make the 3 hour drive to my friend's place in another part of the province. After driving past our acreage again I had to pull over for another little cry. A familiar truck drove by and caught me mid-cry. Thank goodness that person wouldn't have recognized my new vehicle.

It was a lot, and I have to continually remind myself to give myself some grace. This trip was ripping off the nearly healed scabs and processing new "firsts" again.

Another first happened a week later when I saw one of his family members for the first time.

As soon as he announced our split I was completely disowned by his family. We had become very close over the eight years we were together, and I grieved the loss of them in my life, and felt a strong sense of abandonment by them too.

My friends had bought a smoker from my ex's cousin and he was going to be delivering it to their farm. This cousin had lived just down the street from us, was one of my ex's business partners, and his daughter was the flower girl at our wedding. So we knew each other well. While I was preparing myself emotionally for this encounter, we learned that his uncle would be making the delivery instead. His uncle also lived down the street from us, we had spent a ton of time, we traveled with and was also a part of the family business. So needless to say, I was terrified of how this interaction would go.

When he arrived to make the delivery, I stayed inside to compose myself before heading out to the garage where everyone was. Once I came through the door, I don't think he recognized me right away, and when he did he was extremely surprised to see me there. We exchanged pleasantries, I could tell my presence made him a little uncomfortable. I had to escape inside to have a little cry and wipe away the tears. I came back out and indirectly I learned how his family was doing and what they were up to. We chatted a little bit at the end. It was so sad. He was the same kind, gentle-hearted man I remembered and I wanted so badly to give him a hug and go back to the lake with him like everything was back to normal.

And I still can't get through reading that journal entry without bawling.

My situation was unique in that I really did lose everything in my divorce, tangible and intangible. Except our three dogs, thank God. They stayed with me.

We spent most of our time with his family, so despite trying to split holidays and see mine more often, I became distant from my family and very close with his. I only had a small handful of friends from college that were just my friends, everyone else were our mutual friends, couple friends, or family friends. When he left, my world dramatically shrunk down to acquaintances and malnourished relationships.

Divorce shows you a lot about people. Overnight I lost people that had been my family for nearly a decade, friends that I knew my whole life, and a community I had become so deeply involved with.

Being abandoned by a whole family that I loved and lived life with for my entire adulthood was really tough. Even someone who had been my best friend since I was five years old dumped me. *That was cool.*

Whether people realize it or not, sides are always chosen when a couple split. People forget how to talk to you, they don't know what to say, they spread rumors, believe lies, and share gossip.

My hometown, a small town of 1,800 people that I grew up in and the lake down the road where I spent every summer camping and worked as the park biologist for four years, was also where we built our dream home, where I was on the cottage owners committee, helped kick-start other various community projects, ran the trails, and boated the lake as often as we could. We lived in that same community while we dated and throughout our marriage. My home became our home, there was nothing distinguishing between the two. Because of our separation, that beautiful home and community was tainted by memories of where we were happy. It felt like a twisting dagger.

I felt as though I had lost my place in the world. So I left the place I loved and lived my whole life to avoid the additional hurt that is created when you lose your people—and place—in divorce.

It's funny when you're going through a difficult time how people forget how to talk to you. My community became superficial, with only surface-level conversations or complete ignorance. Because my situation made THEM feel uncomfortable, I was avoided.

Oh, and the rumors. The rumors that did laps around my little hometown still shock me, and I lost a LOT of respect for people who I thought were decent human beings. Of course, these rumors were never said to my face nor was I ever asked if they had any truth. My mom would bring them to me as FYIs of either something her neighbor would ask if it was true or better yet, people stopping her at the post office or on the side of the street reaching for more details to pass around the rumor wheel. I was the talk of the town for months, and in the most unflattering way.

But for those who showed their true colors in the worst ways during this time, were also the ones who proved to be some of the best friends a person could ever be blessed with. These people became my family and tenfold replaced all of those I had lost. This was a powerful lesson in the power of CHOOSING your people, blood or not.

Saying Goodbye

A girlfriend and I in Arizona took full advantage of the Groupon discounts some of our favorite spas would put on around Phoenix and we would plan incredibly affordable monthly spa days together at luxury resorts. I remember it was summer, we booked our spa day that month to be on my wedding anniversary to help distract me from the pain that day represented. We were sitting at the pool, and I knew divorce was inevitable. I hadn't talked to my husband in several months and any interaction we had in the past year gave zero indication that he was coming back. That day felt heavy, for obvious reasons, but my in-laws and all the family I had lost in our split was really bothering me that day, too. I never got the chance to say goodbye to the people who had become family during our marriage. Feeling abandoned and grieving losing them too had been really hard on me.

I tend to be quite symbolic with dates. For example, we got married on our two year dating anniversary. That day, which was our seventh wedding anniversary that I was spending without him, poolside at the Omni MonteLucia Resort and Spa in Scottsdale felt like the appropriate day to say goodbye.

I picked up my phone and in my notes app I started writing a group goodbye letter to my mother and father-in-law, two sister-in-laws, brother-in-law, and my ex's aunt and uncle. People I hadn't spoken to for over a year now, but had been close as family can get during my marriage. For each person, I wrote out how much they meant to me, what I would miss about them, and what I've learned from them that had an impact on me and I would never forget. Some of these people were and still are on my expanders list, and I still love and hold them dearly in my heart.

I debated whether I should send this letter or not, but after talking it through with my girlfriend poolside, it felt right. I needed to do that for me. They were important people in my life and if I was never going to see them again, or interact with them as family I needed to let them know how important they had been to me and give a proper goodbye. So I sent the letter in a group email and included a picture of me and the dogs. Doing right by my morals and values and how I wanted to show up for those relationships, knowing that I would likely never get a reply, felt really good and helped me get the closure I needed.

you don't know what you're
made of until you're forced to
let go of someone you love

r.m. drake

Chapter 11

Feeling Those Firsts

Mantra: *I am brave*

Journal Entry: 22 December 2019

Today I woke up in the strangest mood. I haven't felt this way in a long time. I'm just really sad. I'm sad and I'm mad. It's hard to separate the two feelings and I just can't shake it.

It's a couple days before Christmas, and it's really hitting me how different things are. ***Even though it was technically our second Christmas apart, it was really my first.*** *It's the first Christmas season where it seems real.*

Last Christmas I couldn't even fathom the thought of celebrating the holidays, so I escaped to the beach in Mexico for 10 days. I knocked myself out with Ativan and beachside cocktails so I didn't feel the gaping hole in my heart and soul. I would go to bed before 8pm wearing an eye mask, ear plugs and knocking myself out, again with a sleep aid. I couldn't handle holidays, I couldn't handle happiness. I couldn't handle being alone through it all. So I chose not to, and I feel lucky enough that I didn't have to.

Anyways, long story short, other than the upgraded meal served at the resort buffet, I did not celebrate Christmas or New Years' Eve 2018.

A lot has happened this last year and even though I feel stronger, happier and somewhat put back together, the holidays are still hitting me hard.

I had just gotten back from an impromptu month-long trip mid December, and it took me a good week to get my bearings back after being away for so long. So last night I finally went out and did some Christmas-y stuff. Nothing fancy, I was just meeting friends downtown to see Christmas lights. But as I drove down from my mountain community it hit me just how different things were.

I LOVED loved loved the Christmas holidays. That week-long time of the year when you just ate, drank and had the best quality time with family and friends. Time and space didn't matter, just the people. There was no other time of the year like it and we truly celebrated it.

We had created so many fun traditions together. Eight years of Christmas traditions. My whole adult life was Christmas-ing with him, with us as a family. Man do I ever miss it.

Now, it's all gone. And I'm here in a strange house, in a new place trying to make a go of it on my own. Making my own traditions which, right now, are bringing more sadness than happiness. I want my old life back.

This is not how it's supposed to be. I don't recognize anything—which I know is exactly what I wanted when I moved here—but it amplifies what is no more.

Not only did I lose my husband, I lost everything that ever mattered to me. My family, my friends, my home, our traditions, what we built together. It all got bulldozed over and lit to flames. There aren't even ashes left over because it was such a catastrophic nuclear disaster that any trace of what was just disappeared.

I feel like such a stranger in the life I am currently living because everything that I had known was taken away from me.

The holidays suck more, because that's when you're really reminded that you're the outcast and they're still living the life you were a part of for so long.

That's why I was mad.

I burst into tears. An uncontrollable sob that went on for over an hour until I called my mom to help calm me down.

Nothing about this year's Christmas looked or felt the same. I was so completely mad and utterly heartbroken upon realizing this.

I'd miss Christmas tree hunting in the bush to find our perfect tree. I'd miss snowmobiling to the Green Lake shack on Boxing Day to meet up with our neighbors and friends at the lake. I'd miss my mother-in-law's amazing cooking. I'd miss Christmas caroling around our subdivision, singing in exchange for homemade eggnog. I'd miss all of the friends I'd get to reunite with at the lake. I'd miss seeing my in-laws who would come together from out of town who I had grown so close with. I'd miss my sister-in-law sneaking scuffles into Christmas Eve mass and making us all stifle our giggles.

And everyone else got to carry on living out our holiday traditions —except me.

Even if I decided to go back home to spend it with my family, he took that away from me, too. My hometown was our hometown and where we lived for the majority of our marriage. It's filled with so many memories of our life together that would be way too much to bear, especially around Christmas.

I cried and cried. It hurt so much, this was like another heartbreak because I was actually grieving these memories for the first time.

Time is something no one understands when going through separation or divorce. Time passes but the emotions can still be just as strong as the first time you felt them.

This is the grace I have to give myself this holiday season. There are no rules around my grieving. Nearly a year and a half later I'm still getting triggered by the littlest of things.

I spent eight years, my entire adult life, making memories and loving someone I thought I'd spend my life with. Every facet of my existence had involved him. That doesn't just go away.

If my pain is directly correlated to the amount of love I felt, I am truly blessed and cannot regret having loved so hard for it to hurt this much.

I think in this instance, you just gotta miss them. You're allowed to miss them, miss the things, the people, the traditions.

A little while back I watched Eat Pray Love for the first time. I never really got on the hype when it first came out, probably because it was meant for the moment I needed to really hear Elizabeth Gilbert's story. There was an exchange in that movie between Liz and a friend that really resonated with me, and it's stuck with me since.

Liz: "But I love him."

Friend: "So love him."

Liz: "But I miss him."

Friend: "So miss him. Send him some love and light every time you think about him, then drop it. You're just afraid to let go of the last bits of David because then you'll be really alone, and Liz Gilbert is scared to death of what will happen if she's really alone."

I'm allowed to still love these people. I'm allowed to miss them.

*What I've found throughout this whole process is to really allow myself to **feel** those thoughts. To take a couple of minutes to really love them, to really miss them. Then move on. Not dwell in it.*

'I'm still learning. Learning to observe my thoughts and feelings. To understand them, where they're coming from. One thing that is taking me a long time is to learn how to control my feelings. We have that control, I am not my thoughts.

Practicing it is hard. But what we feel and think is a choice - so learn to control it, because really. That's the only way to help move through and survive.

Every little thing I experienced for the first time post-separation had a sting to it. It wasn't something I got used to, and it surprised me every time how much it still hurt. Heck, nearly five years later and some things still catch me off guard when I feel that old familiar stab.

But again, let yourself feel the pain. Don't run from it because that's what keeps it churning inside.

Apart from the Christmas holidays, here were some of my most difficult moments:

Seeing **"Separated" and then "Divorced"** on my Income Tax Returns. *Why you gotta label me like that?*

The first time I was asked if I was married or single. I was going through the border control customs in Peru December 2019 where you obviously can't lie. Quite plainly, the officer asked me if I was married or single. It took me a second to reply. All of my senses instinctively went to my ring finger that was now bare. I swallowed and instead directed all of my energy on the ring on my middle finger, my ring for me. My ring of strength. I gathered up all my courage as a separated woman, either single nor divorced, and said "Ugh, no I'm single."

The officer simply smiled and carried on to the next question. Little did he know the complete torment that was going on inside. After I was approved I walked down the hall and found a little wall jut-out to hide behind and had a little cry. The first time having to say it out loud felt so wrong.

The first time I had to refer to him as my ex-husband. That shift from WE to ME took a lot of work in how I spoke about myself and my story. I didn't start calling him my ex-husband until we were divorced, so that was a first that came over a year and a half into our separation.

The first family death. It was January 2023 when I learned that my ex's grandfather passed away. My ex was very close with his grandfather and we spent quite a bit of time with him throughout our marriage. It felt like I had lost a grandparent, and I grieved, wishing I could be with "my family" during this time. That was tough.

I felt like I had to reach out, I couldn't not. But would my good intentions be taken the wrong way? You never know how things could be perceived after all this time had passed. Ultimately, I decided my soul wouldn't feel right if I didn't at least send a card. I bought sympathy cards for each of the family members and wrote personal messages of my deepest condolences, even a personalized one to him. Some of the aunts thanked me for the message, and it felt really good to hear from them. Some of the letters I didn't end up sending, because after writing it out I realized sending my thoughts and love from afar was just the same.

Dating apps. They are horrible. Engaging in these mainly came out of loneliness. I didn't know where to start because the last time I dated there were no dating apps. I downloaded Match and after getting my first and very forward message I freaked out and instantly emailed Match begging for a refund. It was just too intense right out of the gates.

Going on a date. Let's just say that when the guy wanted to cuddle on the couch and watch a movie, this felt WAY too intimate for me. I left shortly into the date, cried my whole way home, and had to stop to puke on the side of the road. *Good job, Steph.*

First time catching feelings. This didn't happen to me for a long time and it took a handful of dates until I wouldn't cry afterwards or get ghosted before I found someone that I genuinely wanted to go on multiple dates with. He was incredibly sweet, thoughtful, and planned the best dates I have ever been on. We saw each other for just over a month. He was a great catch, but didn't want the same things as me and I knew I couldn't just do casual dating—I would get too attached. So once I started catching feelings we decided it was best to not see each other anymore. And honestly, this was a big part of getting to know myself. I knew myself enough that I couldn't just casually date and that by seeing this guy that was just not aligned with what I wanted in life, I was ultimately setting myself up for heartbreak. Also, dating someone who isn't aligned with what you want just blocks out any possibilities of men who do want the same things. This was a very gentle way of breaking into the dating realm. I decided to choose myself over in-the-moment loneliness and short term intimacy.

we fall. we break. we fail.
but then, we rise, we heal,

we overcome

Chapter 12

Forgiveness

Mantra: *I am worthy*

Just like the word acceptance, I struggle a LOT with the word forgiveness. Just like the word love they are often thrown carelessly, and are often mistaken as a gloss over term that everything is okay.

The term forgive is defined in Webster's dictionary as: to stop feeling angry or resentful toward (someone) for an offense, flaw, or mistake.

And by that definition, I do not forgive. I was (and still am) angry. Forgiveness, by that definition to me, makes it seem like what happened was okay, that the issue is minimized to less than its full weight. To forgive felt like a betrayal to myself and the pain I went through.

I still resent the actions that were taken that hurt me. I still resent the person who made them who was the one person who was never supposed to hurt me like that, and I still resent the friends and family who left me when my life was falling apart.

Those are now just facts and pieces of my story, and they no longer have gripping control over me, but in the traditional definition I do not forgive them or those actions.

Most of the coaches, therapists, and friends that I talked to about forgiveness all encouraged me to forgive for MY sake. Forgiving them is not for them, it's for me to get peace to move on. Of course I wanted that release from the pain that had a tight grip over every essence of my being but not at the cost of making what happened seem okay.

I fought this for quite a while. It didn't feel right until I came across one quote that allowed me to finally forgive in a way that felt true to me. My social media algorithms were fine tuned to give me the encouraging messages and relatable material I needed to hear. Despite the ridiculousness that happens on TikTok, I did come across some really valuable clips.

One in particular was by by user @growingtoloveme that transcribed to say:

"Forgiveness is giving up the hope that the past could be any different. ... You think forgiving means accepting what has happened to you. Well, it is accepting that it HAS happened to you, not accepting that it was okay for it to happen. It is accepting that it has happened, and now "what do I do about it?"

Forgiving is giving up the hope, not holding on, wishing that it could have been any other way than it actually was. **Giving up the hope that the past could be any different.** It's letting go so that the past does not hold you prisoner, does not hold you hostage.

I resonate so deeply with that. It is that definition of forgiveness that I practice now, even though it took me a couple years to subscribe to.

For over 10 months after he left I held on to the slightest chance he would change his mind and come back to us (me and the dogs). I held on to that hope for a number of reasons, mainly my love and compassion for the man I once knew. It wasn't until I learned that he was moving on that I released that hope.

The first person who ever shared this opinion of forgiveness with me was a therapist in Victoria, which is likely why she was my longest running therapist. We do not have to forgive. We do not have to release any anger or resentment—especially if someone else is telling us we should. I mean, you can if you want to. I don't want to stay angry but it is still an emotion that I experience when I think back to my past. But I can and have released the hope that my past could have turned out differently.

Shamanism also doesn't believe in forgiveness, but it believes in acceptance which, by definition, is the ability to acknowledge the reality of a situation without resistance. Accept what has happened and be thankful for the lessons it's taught you—that got you to where you are today.

I was visiting my cousin's house about 10 months after he left, and in catching up they nonchalantly mentioned that my ex had moved on. Learning that shook my soul. I was crushed. We were still technically married, separated but not yet divorced, and I died inside.

That was the night I took off my engagement ring. I kept my wedding band on, but the engagement ring held so much more emotion. I had an emergency call with my coach, Ava. I needed some help to process, to breathe. It was then she introduced me to a version of the Hawaiian Prayer for Forgiveness. Despite my feelings around forgiveness, this prayer encompasses my outlook on this whole experience of divorce—the hardest life lesson I've ever had to learn. It's called the Ho'oponopono Prayer.

> *I'm sorry you had to do this for me to grow.*
>
> *Please forgive me for bringing out that side of you.*

Thank you for teaching me this lesson.

I love you, because we are all one.

That night I asked my cousin to use her tub and took a long, hot bath. I must have been in there for at least two hours and repeated ho'o-ponopono over and over and over again. Crying for so long I had used up all my tears, and there was just a jerking sob coming from within.

What I love the most about this version of ho'oponopono that Ava shared with me, is that its an expanded version of anything I've seen online:

I'm sorry

Please Forgive Me

Thank you

I love you.

Ava's version turns any situation—whether I'm saying the prayer about others or MYSELF when I need a little extra grace, into a universal lesson of human experience. Where forgiveness meets us at the raw level of our inner child seeing another inner child reacting in a sometimes unfair world and understanding that we all make mistakes. This prayer got me through many, many nights, and helped me meet my ex at a soul level of his true core that I fell in love with and forgiving that piece of him.

she silently stepped out of the
race that she never wanted to
be in, found her own lane and
proceeded to *win*

Chapter 13

Funeral for My Past

Mantra: *My past does not define me*

Journal Entry: August 18, 2021

It's the day. The day that for the longest time was the happiest day of my life now turned into one of the saddest days of my life.

Healing is not linear and it has no timeline. Overwhelming emotions can sneak up and take over, and I've learned to let them.

It's hard to breathe. I can't stop crying. and I'm just incredibly sad and caught up in such a deep grief that I can't exactly pinpoint what I'm grieving.

It's a combination of things.

Grieving a life that I loved and lost.

Grieving a person who I thought was my person, and who I should be spending today with - and every other day.

Grieving the future I thought I'd have, but never got to live.

The stabbing pain of rejection and abandonment take control.

Today acts like a big highlighter on all the hurt I've been through.

The last 6 months or so the only feeling I've felt towards him and what happened has been anger. So feeling this sadness again just sucks.

I thought I was past this. But I know it's a part of the process

My therapist has constantly reminded me how relatively recent our divorce still is, and how I have to give myself grace for this process.

We've only been divorced a year and a half, and I was still fully committed to my marriage the year and a half of separation prior to the papers coming through.

All in all, a year and a half divorced I've been doing pretty darn good.

So today, I'm allowed to be sad. and I'm going to let myself feel all the feels.

—---

It was November 2020, and his birthday was mid-month. Still to this day the birthdays and anniversaries weigh on me. On those days I try to be extra gentle with myself, plan to do something special for myself, and let it be what it will be.

That year I just felt tired of the hurt and the pain. So I planned a "Funeral for My Past," inspired by some work from Gabrielle Bernstein and the song *Funeral For My Past* by Liz Longley.

The day of his birthday I drove out to the coast. I was living on Vancouver Island at the time and spent a lot of time on the beaches between Sooke and Port Renfrew. I went to my favorite beach, Sandcut Beach. There were intense waves from a tapering off storm crashing onto the beach dragging back the rocks making a light "tinkling" sound that was quite meditative and soothing. Everything about this place is pure magic. The dogs and I hiked down through a magical temperate rainforest where bright green ferns cover the forest floor highlighting the red dirt, and bare trunks reach high into the sky creating a thick canopy. The air is so fresh, slightly scented by the surrounding cedar in this old growth forest and salty shoreline just down the path. When we get to the beach after about a 400 meter hike down, the forest opens up into the most picturesque, rugged west coast beach. To the right the beach is a beautiful light sand that curves around a bay. To the left the beach is rocky with some large rock jut outs.

The pups and I head left down the rocky beach, where the rough waves have carved out a steep drop off. My favorite part of this beach is a little bit of a way down, where a creek meets the ocean by running off a slick rock, creating a little waterfall before running into the ocean. I settle down on a big piece of driftwood and let the dogs run about. They love swimming in the freshwater pool at the bottom of the little waterfall, even though it is frigid in mid-November.

I brought along my journal and turned to a new page. Gabby Bernstein's *Miracle Membership* offered monthly workshops and exercises and that month felt so fitting for today's "funeral." It was a releasing activity where you write down on a small piece of paper what is stressing you out or bothering you, then you fold it up and either bury, dispose, or burn the paper symbolizing releasing whatever you wrote down.

My version of the exercise consisted of writing down every hurtful, dismissive, and minimizing thing that happened throughout my marriage, separation, and divorce. These were words that haunted me, that made me feel an inch tall, that made me feel unworthy, rejected, abandoned, and unloved. I wrote down what I lost, what I was grieving, and the pain I had been carrying with me. After each line of hurtful words or situations, I would rewrite it into something empowering or loving.

For example:

"I don't love you anymore" would be rewritten into, "I don't need your love to complete me."

This took up nearly two pages. I cried as people walked past me on the beach and my dogs jumped up on me to lick my tears away. I held nothing back. I allowed myself to grieve like I was at a funeral.

I grieved the man I fell in love with, the home we built, the future we planned. I grieved for the 29 year old version of myself who became a shell of a person having to pick up the glass shards of her heart and life and figure out how to put them back together. I grieved for all the tears I cried, anti-depressant pills I took, and how I was forever changed.

And then I just kept journaling on all the hard things we had gone through together and all the harder things I had gone through since he left. What I would say to him at that moment. It all came flowing out. I was taking my power back.

I played the song "Funeral for My Past" and really felt the lyrics. I even wrote them down, line by line.

I brought a lighter along, and I tore the sheets out of my journal, lit them on fire, and watched them burn. Releasing those thoughts, words, and emotions through the smoke and into the wind.

let whatever you do today

be enough

Chapter 14

Mental Health is Not for the Weak

Mantra: *I am beautiful, inside and out*

Blog Post: January 5, 2020

I survived 2019 - and I don't say that lightly.

When I didn't think things could get any worse, they became unimaginably horrible. When I didn't think someone could hurt me any more, my heart broke even more into an irreparable mess.

There were days when it hurt too much to go on and awake was the last place I wanted to be. All the antidepressants in the world could not have - and did not - help me during this time.

It's really crazy to think about how much has changed in a year.

The beginning of 2019 was so vastly different than it is now.

January 1, 2019 the only thing I wanted (other than my husband to come back) was to feel something other than heartbreak, rejection and abandonment. The pain was so all-encompassing that it would literally take the breath out of me.

I was so completely and utterly broken.

For months and months I ran from my emotions. If I couldn't distract myself I would numb myself. Thank God for red wine and a strong edible.

I wasn't out partying, drinking, hooking up. Thats not me. Travel was my main distraction. Six countries, six provinces, five states, 27 destinations and more planes than I can count distracted me from my reality for the last 12 months. And when I wasn't on an airplane I was on the comfiest couch in the world in my living room with the blinds drawn binge-watching Netflix and crushing pints of edible cookie dough.

I don't know what I did with my time, and time went by very slowly. Amplifying what was going on in my life. If I wasn't working I was sleeping, or watching TV. Not much else.

Working from home turned me into a hermit. I did not need to leave my house - so I rarely did. Most day's I didn't change out of my PJ's and Postmates delivered all of my meals. My poor dogs were confined to our backyard and were rarely walked.

I had zero energy but I couldn't sleep. My hormones were so messed up I was in extreme adrenal fatigue.

My grief had taken over every facet of my life.

And just when I thought I was doing "ok", I would find out something he was doing. And it would kill me all over again. Like a knife stabbing into my heart over and over and over.

I don't think the pain ever got less. I just learned to live with it. Some days I'd take a step ahead, others 10 steps back. So I learned to just take things day by day.

Slowly, I picked up my pieces and started to put myself together again.

Time wasn't on my side in 2019. But I know now that I needed to live through that pain, like a slow death, to be reborn again.

Thankfully, I don't recognize that person from January 1, 2019 anymore.

This last year I experienced some of my darkest moments - but I also created some of my best memories.

- *I started a new job I love.*
- *I checked off so many amazing places on my bucket list.*
- *I bought a house and moved across the country and border back to Canada for a fresh start.*
- *I stood by my best friend on her wedding day.*
- *I saw my other best friends more than I had in the last 3 years.*
- *I turned 30 in Maui.*
- *I shared a fence with a new best friend.*
- *I invested in myself, I dated myself, and I learned to love myself again.*
- *I found my voice and I learned my worth.*
- *I set boundaries to keep my peace of mind and maintain my self-respect.*

I have so many things to be grateful for and learned so many priceless lessons.

What I've learned through this time in my life I wouldn't change for anything because it's brought me here. To this person (myself) and this place.

I survived <3

It's no surprise after reading more than half of this book that I truly struggled. I am so proud of myself for climbing out of that dark hole of depression and despair because it was not easy. I know it's an overused saying, but I literally just put one foot in front of another and didn't focus on anything past the present.

Mental health is not for the weak, and it is greatly undermined. I was the first (and only one) in my family to be open about experiencing depression, and when I was brave enough to share I was told to just be stronger.

I battled, and still battle, daily with myself.

If you are feeling similar thoughts, there is nothing wrong with you. Mental illnesses are imbalances in our brain chemistry that make us feel that way. We are not our mental illness just like we are not our divorce. It's the same as a broken bone or sprained ankle where we need to see the doctor for help. It's nothing shameful, and it's nothing we have control over. It does NOT make you less than or weak. The battles going on within us take a lot of fight.

You are strong, you are powerful, and you have a beautiful mind. Don't forget that.

throw her to the flames and

she'll become like fire

Chapter 15

When You're Ready

Mantra: *My heart is open*

It's unfortunate how many people feel like it's helping to tell you what you should do to feel better, especially if they don't know how you're really feeling. Which is impossible, because every relationship, separation, and divorce is unique and can only be properly handled by **you**. No one else has the information you have, lived through your moments, or felt what you felt. So honestly, they don't get a say. When you're ready, you'll know.

Wedding Rings

It was either my second or third day at the SpiritQuest retreat, and I was meeting with a new practitioner, let's call her Marg. Marg was older, maybe mid to late fifties, short grey hair, and sharp features. She was honestly kind of intimidating and not nurturing at all. Her session was themed around acceptance and helping me move on. Other practitioners had done guided meditations, like the cord-cutting meditation with me to start to sever some of my attachment to my husband. Marg wanted to take a more bold approach. She asked me why I was still wearing my wedding rings. *Dude my husband just suddenly left me only three months ago, we're just formally separated as of a week ago, and even though we're separated that means we are STILL married. Which means I am wearing my wedding rings.*

She was confused by my answer and adamant that taking off my rings would help me.

She then led me into a guided meditation. In the meditation she guided me down a wooded trail following a river, and at the river was my husband. There was a table, what looked like a golden altar like the ones found in Catholic churches. It was covered in a white cloth with a golden plate on it. Then Marg said to me in the meditation "He wants you to take off your rings, he says it's time."

I instantly opened my eyes and said in a harsh tone "Fuck that. Absolutely not" and I walked out of the session. I then told the office what happened and asked that any future sessions with Marg be rescheduled to another practitioner.

She had no right bringing me into that meditation and using my husband to get me to take my rings off. I was furious.

I confided in another practitioner what happened and how upset I was. She was much gentler and compassionate, and shared her own story of divorce and her wedding rings.

Your wedding rings and bands were a gift and a promise given by someone out of love. They were a gift to you, they're yours, and represent **your** love and commitment that you hold in your marriage and relationship—no one else's. Not even your spouse. When this other practitioner felt like it was time for her to take off her rings, she replaced them with a ring she bought herself, and wore that ring on her ring finger as a symbol that she loved herself and wasn't ready for a relationship with anyone else.

It wasn't until six months later, so nearly ten months into my separation, when I took my engagement ring off. After a lot of thought and tears, I decided it was time. I held a ritual that comprised of my favorite self-care practice, prayers, and an understanding with God that I was taking my rings off because I was finally letting go of hope. I took off my engagement ring and wedding band but left on my third band (I had a set of three) as a symbol that I was still married and still committed to the vow I made on my wedding day. I was still holding up my end of our commitment.

Two months later I took off the third band, because looking at it was making me feel sick and became triggering. But when I took it off I was even more upset by a bare hand. So I bought myself my own ring, just as my Sedona practitioner had done for herself. I didn't put it on my ring finger though, that didn't feel right to me. I instead decided to wear it on my middle finger on my left hand so every time I felt the lightness on that now bare ring finger I would look down and see my own diamonds that I bought myself.

Now everytime I look down at my left hand I am reminded of how strong, resilient, brilliant, and beautiful I am and my journey back to myself in that ring.

Ladies, we can buy our own diamonds.

Shared Last Name

When I married, I hyphenated my last name keeping my maiden name and adding my married name to the end. I was proud of my accomplishments as the single "Steph Leis," but informally went by just my married name after our wedding. Formally I was Stephanie Leis-Hudye.

I kept going by just "Steph Hudye" for a long time. I grew so much as that person, that was me. I had that name for six years, I wasn't "Steph Leis" anymore. It was weird though that I was triggered by seeing just that last name by itself, but when I saw it in my name, it felt right. I was given that name by my ex, but that name had also become me. Steph Hudye was a woman of integrity. She never gave up on love, she stood by her morals and values. I was so proud of everything that woman went through.

But also Steph Hudye was changing, and Valentines Day 2020, as I sat alone at home crushing chocolate and red wine, I decided it was time. I made the first official "change" on my social media, although I was kind of annoyed there was now another "Steph Leis" in the world that was hogging all the good handles. Slowly I changed my name on my email signature, my work slack account, and other random places I came about over time. I never did change my formal last name, I am still Stephanie Leis-Hudye, and that last name still catches me off guard when I look at it the wrong way. But that's me. And it's also way too much work to change my passport and banking info.

You Love Again

Now I don't write this from experience, but rather hope and SCREAMING it out to the universe that I am ready for my new husband.

I don't know when the switch turned on, how many meditations, the number of EFT tapping sessions, or times I wrote out my future-husband manifestations, but eventually I was ready to open my heart up again. That doesn't mean it wasn't scary AF, because it still is. And I have to consciously remember to put my guard down. But LOVE is what carried me through my separation and divorce. LOVE is and always will be worth it, no matter how much it might hurt sometimes. I will never regret how I loved wholeheartedly and unconditionally, and I can't imagine leading a life that isn't in love.

I know my pain and heartbreak was a direct correlation to how much I loved. So I will never regret that.

Two manifesting tools I love to use, as I call-in my future husband, are guided manifesting meditations and writing a very specific list of the qualities, characteristics, and even physical appearance I desire in him. I've written out this list SO many times, I've become extremely clear in what I DO what, and what I DON'T want. It's not being picky, I just have new standards now.

For the last three years I've been having the same vision during my manifesting meditation. I'm on my favorite beach on Maui, Ka'anapali Beach. It's sunset. I'm looking down at my bare feet in the sand with a white linen dress skirting my ankles. In the distance I hear "Come on, Mommy" and I look up and see three figures up ahead. I can't see them too clearly, but there is a tall man with dark hair smiling and holding the hand of two littles. A little girl with curly dark blonde hair in a white dress waving to me, and a little boy, in a white shirt and tan shorts, also with a curling blonde mop on his head being held by his dad. I run up to them. We all embrace, holding each other, spinning gently in a circle. I can feel them hugging me, smell the sweet salty air, and feel the last warm rays of the sunset hitting our cheeks. We then sit down on the beach, and my husband and I watch the kids play in the sand. It is a true paradise.

I'm still waiting for this dream man to arrive. But I now have every faith in God that I deserve a man like this, a family like this, and he will come at the right time and when I am ready for him. Which is why I wholeheartedly believe doing the work, healing from my trauma, is necessary before I can truly step into my future.

But in the meantime dating has been... challenging to say the least.

Journal Entry: January 25, 2020

I could probably write a whole book about the AWFUL dates I've been on. I curse myself for laughing all those years ago when I was married about how I could never survive the dating scene and dating apps these days—Thank God I was married! Karma, you bitch.

Dating is a whole different ballpark since the last time I was single over a decade ago. It's stressful, full of games, and is super unnerving. Dating apps are the most awkward thing ever but a necessary evil because how else do people meet during while living busy adult lives, never mind during a pandemic.

Here's the best of the best:

- *The guy who drank out of our uber driver's water bottle. Gross.*
- *The guy who did ecstatic dancing, with light up mittens for finger dancing. He also used to be a grocery store produce manager, would talk to the fruits and veggies, and felt SO sorry for the old produce that got thrown away it would bring him to tears. Nope, can't do that.*
- *The guy who took me elk scouting and made me examine bear scat. Why tho.*
- *The guy who practiced his comedy set on me and wished he had a pet sugar glider that he kept in his shirt pocket. Wtf.*
- *The guy who forgot to tell me he had a girlfriend. Ugh.*
- *The 5 foot cop that I towered over in heels who waved me across the street like a traffic director. Thanks for keeping me safe, I guess.*
- *The guy who talked like a surfer while wearing a sweater vest. No thanks.*
- *The guy who lived in a van, used me for a hot shower and comfy bed, AND didn't tell me his real name #nottyler*
- *The guy with a penis shaped tree stump in his yard, that he carved himself.*

These strange, curious creatures have kept life interesting.

But in all seriousness, it's been a huge season of learning patience, letting go of control, and putting all my faith in God that the ones who leave aren't meant to be and the right one will come at the right time, when I'm ready and when he's ready.

A TikTok I saw last night said "He left for a reason. You prayed for a good man, and he wasn't it sis."

And dang, did that ever hit.

Dear future husband... Where you at? I'm waiting, but not very patiently.

and bless the thing that broke you
down and cracked you open because
the world needs you open

rebecca campbell

Chapter 16

Listen for the Lessons

Mantra: *I am exactly where I need to be*

Journal Entry: November 5, 2021

It's funny how many roles my ex played in my life.

Not only did our separation and divorce absolutely destroy me—but he also showed me what real love is.

Our first six years together he set the standard of what I want in my next relationship and how I deserve to be treated. I was his queen and he treated me like one. I felt like the luckiest woman in the world. The last three years together, well, he showed me exactly what I do not want. But I now have boundaries, non-negotiables and standards set on both sides of the spectrum.

A truth I found during my separation was that lessons can be found in every experience we have, positive or negative. That lesson might be like sticking your hand on a hot stove top saying "I'll never do that again" or taking the wrong turn on the freeway and finding a gem of a coffee shop leaving you thinking "Huh, I would have never experienced the best coffee I've ever drank if this unexpected detour never happened." Life can be funny that way by showing us the beauty in the unexpected and sometimes shitty stuff. Our life experiences and lessons then create filters of how we move forward and see our world. Some lessons we need to learn multiple times before they stick, others can completely change the trajectory of our lives.

My separation and divorce forever changed me. It is a huge part of my life that left such an impact and led me down a path I never wanted, but one I had to learn to live with. Although I have now built a life I love, one that feels authentic and true to me, I am not grateful for what happened that led me to this point of empowerment. I would give anything to go back to my previous life, because I didn't choose this one. This happened out of pure default. I had no other choice if I wanted to survive.

These are are some of the biggest lessons I learned that helped me survive that hell:

- I found myself again.
- I found my voice.
- I remembered my morals and values.
- I know what I stand for.
- I know what I deserve.
- I have a new-found confidence in my unique self.
- I have boundaries and standards.
- I know exactly what I want out of life, and I'm not afraid to go after it.

Whatever we resist, persists. Embrace the pain. Don't run from it. Sit with it. Let it teach you. You have to feel it to release it. Listen for those lessons, and watch them turn into some of your greatest gifts.

you've got a new story to write,

and it looks nothing like your past

danielle laporte

Chapter 17

Writing Your Next Chapter

Mantra: *I rise above*

Journal Entry: April 30, 2022

Everything is Figure-out-able 🤍

My mantra while I am continually hit with challenges, obstacles, and nothing seems to be in my favor. Be adaptable, pivot, take the lesson, move on.

Before moving from Scottsdale to Victoria I met with one of my girlfriends for coffee, and after a beautiful good-bye visit she gifted me a keyring that said *"Now is your time to shine."* To this day I still have that key ring on my vehicle keys. In this season of separation, darkness is referenced often, and I've held close the analogy of "finding the light" as I was climbing my way out of depression. The "light" at the end of the tunnel is what will keep you moving forward day by day and transitioning into "shining your light" is what will help you thrive.

Letting your light shine and speaking your truth serves the world. That's why I'm here sharing this book with you. Our vulnerability, authenticity, and genuineness during a time of struggle can empower those silently suffering.

You are not alone. Even though it feels that way. Even though you lost your person. You will be okay. There's no shame in what you're going through or feeling. You don't have to hide it. As humans we crave connection, and connecting through struggle can be a beautiful way to build community with those who have shared experiences. Some of my best tools, mantras and ideas have come from people and places where I've least expected. They've given me little nuggets of wisdom that have blossomed into the most incredible experiences and realizations.

I refer to these tools and resources now as my "medicine". They're what lift me up, change my perspective, and bring me peace when I need it the most. I hope that my own special "medicine" concoction of mantras, experiences, lessons, and practices help you navigate whatever journey you're on as well.

I want to leave you with my best piece of advice. Have zero regrets. Live through this time intentionally. Keep loving hard. Love was the forefront of every action I took in my separation, whether it was for myself or my soon to be ex spouse, I kept loving. True love doesn't judge. True love has no conditions. All you can do is accept, forgive and love.

Today, as I'm finishing up this dream of writing this book for you, it's been five years, one month and 29 days since he left. Being completely honest, I'm still figuring it out and it still scares the shit out of me sometimes.

Everytime a first date goes bad, I curse my ex-husband because he put me in the situation of being single. I lived through my first wildfire sweeping through my beautiful new city, and it was terrifying experiencing that alone. Any time I have something to celebrate, my mind instinctively still goes to sharing it with him. I still have some really shitty days where I don't get out of bed, and my biological clock ticks so loudly it's hard to sleep at night thinking how badly I want to be a mother. And I curse him again for taking my best reproductive years. It sucks and it will for a while. Happy moments will catch you off guard with sad intrusive thoughts and there'll be days when all you want is your old life back. I feel you, and I am so so sorry you have to go through this too. But know you are not alone.

Even though I haven't found my next big, forever love, I've found love in different ways, shapes, and forms that fill me up for now. I've used my flexible work lifestyle to now be there for my people who were there for me at my lowest points. I still love, but now I put extra love into my dogs and the far too many plants in my house. My best friends have become my family, and I've grown extremely close with their kids by spending Christmas holidays, summers, and vacations with them which brings me more happiness than I ever imagined. They're at the top of my expanders list for what I can't wait for in my future marriage and family. For now, I am choosing to be the best version of myself - to be the best friend, daughter, sister, dog mom, neighbor, colleague, contractor, etc. etc. etc. I can be - until its my turn to have it all. I am making this precious time count and I hope you can too.

Love always wins—if you choose it.

so what's next?

you heal,
you grow
and you help others

Epilogue

Mantra: *I am letting myself bloom*

Journal Entry: 28 October 2023

Today I've finished the final edits of my book that will be published and released to the world in just a few short weeks. What a journey it's been. As I sit here in my living room, on the couch with the fireplace on, overlooking the gorgeous Okanagan valley, sipping a glass of wine, surrounded by my little fur family, I am overcome with pride. I am so, so proud of how far I have come. I wish Steph five years ago could have known that we would be ok. That would we would not only survive, but thrive. That there was a power and magic inside of us that was just waiting to be released and that our story, this parable of a broken heart, could help others in a way we needed most.

I am so grateful for the woman I have become. For how resilient and strong I am. I am grateful that I can now look in the mirror and feel the love that I have created within myself. Where I am whole, without needing to look to someone else to complete me. And of course I look forward to the day when I find love again, and I know it is coming, but

I know that it will be with a man who is deserving of me. A man that can meet me where I am now – after all of the ways that I have healed and grown.

All of the tools, techniques, resources, practitioners, facilitators, and my own intuition of knowing what was right for me had transformed me from a shell of a person into my own role model. I have created my own home. I am standing, firmly, on my own two feet building a successful business that I love by working with world class leaders, traveling the world, pouring deeply into my people and creating new, potent, and powerful friendships that will last a lifetime. Most of all, I have a peace in my heart knowing and trusting that everything happens for a reason and everything is right on time. Just like taking nearly four years to finish this book. Divine timing is no coincidence and I am planting seeds for my future knowing that this is just the beginning of my next chapter and honoring those who I am fortunate enough to inspire along the way.

Every parable that we share has a powerful lesson and a potent ending that allows us to see the world through a different lens. A broken heart does the same. It gives us a different perspective on life, and if we give ourselves permission to lean into the possibility that a broken heart could be the opening of a new door to a new beginning, a new way of being, a new way of life that truly is meant for you. It's there for you to have and it is so worth fighting for.

Acknowledgments

I don't know where I would be without my people.

To my **mom,** for being there for me when I was at the bottom, and taking care of me when I couldn't. For helping me with the dogs to allow me to heal through travel and have some freedom to find me again.

To my **dad,** for moving me across the country and an international border countless times. For always fixing things, being on the other end of the phone, and looking out for me and the pups.

To **Jorden**, for being exactly who you are.

To **Ebony**, for being my person. For all of the phone calls and visits. You made me feel loved and showed me the true meaning of friendship. Your words of encouragement and strength are more appreciated than you'll ever know. Thank you, from the bottom of my heart. Thank you. And, thank you to you and **Jeff** for adopting me into your family, including me in your holidays, family vacations, and your children's lives. I love you all so much.

To **Ava.** My catalyst.

To **Beau, Finn, and Gracie**. My family, my babies, my protectors. You have been my constants through it all. You lived these stories with me that now the rest of the world knows.

To my **Paradigm Ladies,** for your support, love, and showing me the power of vulnerability.

To **Kim**, for always being the first person I call, the best travel partner, and just seeing me.

To **Lauren**. My Arizona family and shoulder to cry on when I needed to be held. Jenny the Duck forever.

To **Anna**, for bringing so much life and laughter to such a dark period of time in my life. No fence will ever be the same without you on the other side.

Resources

Visit parableofabrokenheart.com/resources for digital versions of the tools, practices, prayers, resources, my spotify playlist and more <3

About the Author

Steph Leis is a dog mom, outdoor enthusiast, and event producer. *Parable of a Broken Heart* is a passion project stemming from a life-shattering divorce that completely changed the trajectory of her life. Having to rebuild from the ground up, Steph has created a life more beautiful and authentic than she could have ever dreamed using the tools and insights shared in this book.

Manufactured by Amazon.ca
Bolton, ON